101 KEY IDEAS

BUDDHISM

101 KEY IDEAS
Buddhism

Mel Thompson

TEACH YOURSELF BOOKS

For UK orders: please contact Bookpoint Ltd, 39 Milton Park, Abingdon, Oxon OX14 4TD. Telephone: (44) 01235 400414, Fax: (44) 01235 400454. Lines are open from 9.00–6.00, Monday to Saturday, with a 24 hour message answering service. Email address: orders@bookpoint.co.uk

For USA & Canada orders: please contact NTC/Contemporary Publishing, 4255 West Touhy Avenue, Lincolnwood, Illinois 60646–1975, USA. Telephone: (847) 679 5500, Fax: (847) 679 2494.

British Library Cataloguing in Publication Data
A catalogue record for this title is available from The British Library.

Library of Congress Catalog Card Number: On file

First published in UK 2000 by Hodder Headline Plc, 338 Euston Road, London, NW1 3BH.

First published in US 2000 by NTC/Contemporary Publishing, 4255 West Touhy Avenue, Lincolnwood (Chicago), Illinois 60646–1975 U.S.A.

Cover illustration and design by Mike Stones.

Typeset by Transet Limited, Coventry, England.
Printed in Great Britain for Hodder & Stoughton Educational, a division of Hodder Headline Plc, 338 Euston Road, London NW1 3BH by Cox & Wyman Ltd, Reading, Berkshire.

Impression number	10 9 8 7 6 5 4 3 2 1
Year	2006 2005 2004 2003 2002 2001 2000

Contents

Introduction

Welcome to the **Teach Yourself 101 Key Ideas** series. We hope that you will find both this book and others in the series to be useful, interesting and informative. The purpose of the series is to provide an introduction to a wide range of subjects, in a way that is entertaining and easy to absorb.

Each book contains 101 short accounts of key ideas or terms which are regarded as central to that subject. The accounts are presented in alphabetical order for ease of reference. All of the books in the series are written in order to be meaningful whether or not you have previous knowledge of the subject. They will be useful to you whether you are a general reader, are on a pre-university course, or have just started at university.

We have designed the series to be a combination of a text book and a dictionary. We felt that many text books are too long for easy reference, while the entries in dictionaries are often too short to provide sufficient detail. The **Teach Yourself 101 Key Ideas** series gives the best of both worlds! Here are books that you do not have to read cover to cover, or in any set order. Dip into them when you need to know the meaning of a term, and you will find a short, but comprehensive account which will be of real help with those essays and assignments. The terms are described in a straightforward way with a careful selection of academic words thrown in for good measure!

So if you need a quick and inexpensive introduction to a subject, **Teach Yourself 101 Key Ideas** is for you. And incidentally, if you have any suggestions about this book or the series, do let us know. It would be great to hear from you.

Best wishes with your studies!

Paul Oliver
Series Editor

A Note on Buddhist Terms

Many terms used in Buddhism are not easy to translate. For example, *Dukkha* – a crucial term for understanding the Buddhist path, and the first of the Four Noble Truths – is sometimes translated as 'suffering', but it doesn't quite mean that. It means something more like 'unsatisfactoriness', a sense that life never quite lives up to our expectations, or the frustration of realizing that even the best and most enjoyable things cannot last for ever. For this reason, many of the key terms are listed in their original language and their meaning is then explained in the text.

Although Japanese, Chinese and Tibetan terms are sometimes found, most of the basic Buddhist terms are either in Pali (an ancient Indian language, similar to that spoken by the historical Buddha and used for the earliest collection of scriptures), or in Sanskrit, the language traditionally used for Indian religion.

Pali and Sanskrit terms are often very similar. For example, *Nirvana* in Sanskrit is *Nibbana* in Pali, *karma* is *kamma*, and so on. Generally speaking, the earlier or more usual term is given in the heading. Where appropriate, both Pali and Sanskrit versions are given in the text.

Abhidhamma

The earliest records of the Buddha's teaching (or *Dhamma*) simply give his response to particular questions and situations. In the early centuries after his death, however, there were various attempts to systematize his teaching, and the books in which these more philosophical and analytic approaches are set out are known as *Abhidhamma* (or 'higher' dhamma). There were a number of Abhidhamma collections, one set in Pali (the language of the earliest collection of Sutras) and another in Sanskrit, which has come down to us through its Chinese translation. In the early Buddhist community there were different schools or traditions of Buddhist philosophy, and these each produced their own Abhidhamma literature. Most of the Abhidhamma literature was written over a period of 500 years, from about 100 BCE.

Whereas the Sutras are relatively straightforward, with the Buddha's teaching set in the context of particular individuals and their questions, the Abhidhamma is detailed, abstract, and far from easy reading.

The Abhidhamma was never intended as an introduction to Buddhism. It is more like a detailed handbook of Buddhist Wisdom for the advanced practitioner. In particular, it aims to deny the notion of a separate, independent self (which Buddhism holds to be at the root of suffering) by constantly analyzing and breaking everything down into its constituent parts, showing it to be 'put together' and temporary.

An important contribution of Abhidhamma is this analysis of self, setting out the basic Buddhist psychology. In particular it sees the self as composed of five *skandhas* or 'heaps' of body, feelings, perceptions, responses and consciousness – recognition of which is a step in appreciating Buddhist spiritual practice.

Confusingly, the atoms of experience – the separate parts of which everything is comprised – are termed dhammas (realities). These are not the same as **the** Dhamma (*Dharma* in Sanskrit) which also means 'reality' and is the term used for the Buddha's teaching.

see also...

Dhamma; Scriptures; Skandhas

Alms Round

This is a frequently misunderstood aspect of the Theravada monastic tradition. Monks take a daily walk – itself an act of meditation – during which they go to a local village or other residential area and receive gifts of food from Buddhist lay people. This is not begging (and the bowls they carry should be referred to as alms bowls, not begging bowls). They are not permitted to ask for food, merely to provide an opportunity, by their presence, for lay people to offer them something.

Receiving alms in this way is in line with the second precept – taking only what is freely given – and provides an opportunity to get to know lay people and strengthen the bond between monks and laity. It has an additional benefit of emphasizing the impermanence of life. Monks cannot plan ahead for their own welfare, they are dependent, day by day, on what others freely choose to give them. They discipline themselves to be detached from what is given, accepting it whether or not it is what they might have chosen to eat. From the lay person's point of view, giving food to the monks is a token of respect for the Sangha, and it is also believed that doing so produces merit (*punya*).

The implication of the alms round is that monks and nuns are not a paid, professional priesthood. There is no contractual or professional relationship between monk and lay person. It is simply a balance, within which the monks offer what they can by way of teaching and help to the lay people, and in return receive what they need.

The very different conditions that prevailed when Buddhism moved northwards into China and Japan meant that the alms round was no longer practicable. Forms of Mahayana Buddhism that developed in the Far East therefore allow their religious leaders to work, handle money and to operate to a far greater extent within secular society.

see also...

Monasticism

Amitabha (Amida)

Amitabha is one of the most commonly found Buddha images in the Far East. He is generally shown with calm, oriental features wearing a simple robe and sitting in meditation. *Amita* means 'infinite' and *abha* is 'light', so Amitabha (or Amida in the Japanese form) is the Buddha of infinite light, to whom many Mahayana Buddhists of the Pure Land schools pay devotion.

There is a tradition that Amitabha Buddha agreed to receive Buddhahood on the condition that he could receive upon their death all who called on his name, transporting them to a Western Paradise, a 'Buddha field' where conditions would be ideal for spiritual development. The *Sukhavati Sutras* describe this ideal land.

Devotion to Amitabha originated in a period in the middle of the first millennium CE, when devotional traditions were gaining in influence in India, both in Hinduism and Buddhism. The emphasis with them was on achieving a personal sense of devotion and love towards one's chosen deity. This was in contrast to the earlier Abhidhamma, which had emphasized the path of analysis and personal exploration.

Later, this form of Buddhism was to be termed 'Pure Land' and was to become a major part of the Buddhist tradition in China and Japan. It is a form of Buddhism that requires no discipline or effort, but only calling on the name of Amitabha. Since Amitabha vows to bring everyone who calls on him to his paradise, morality and religion are not necessary qualifications for success. In many ways, this is radically different in its approach from earlier forms of Buddhism.

Amida is generally portrayed in mandalas (spiritual patterns) as the Buddha of the West. He has associated with the Bodhisattva Avalokiteshvara (the Bodhisattva of Compassion) or the Chinese female equivalent, Kwan-shih-yin, and is the head of the lotus or meditation family of Buddhas.

see also...

Pure Land Buddhism

Anatta (no permanent self)

In traditional Indian thought, the Atman (self) was permanent, distinct from the physical body and capable of passing from life to life. It was the true essence of a person, separable from experiences and actions performed in the present, and ultimately identified with Brahma, the supreme reality. By contrast, the Buddha taught that there is no such eternal self. In fact, everything lacked inherent existence. For convencience, we may divide up what we experience into separate pieces, but in fact they are part of an ongoing stream of physical and mental existence. This is a key feature of Buddhist philosophy.

Everything arises in dependence upon causes and conditions (*paticcasamupada*) and is therefore impermanent. Equally, everything is put together by those causes and conditions, so it does not have an eternal or essential nature. As far as human beings are concerned, each person is made up of five separate bundles or *skandhas* (the physical body, feelings, experience, habitual responses and consciousness), and each of these is constantly changing.

Of course, Buddhists continue to talk about people as individuals, each with his or her own personality, and about individual things as though separate and permanent. If they did not, life at a conventional level would be impossible. But at a deeper level, they recognize that the names we give to things and people *are* simple conventional, and that absolute reality is quite different.

For example, I may know that everything is composed of atoms, themselves analyzable into atomic forces that are invisible and insubstantial. You and I are simply a collection of atoms, molecules and cells, arranged in a very complex and temporary way through instructions contained in our DNA. That is absolute reality: it doesn't stop us having names, but it does remind us of how we are linked to the rest of the universe.

see also...

Interconnectedness

Arhats

Having achieved enlightenment himself, the Buddha spent the remainder of his life teaching others. As a result, many of them are described as having become enlightened and, in this, their experience and insight was not qualitatively different from that of the Buddha himself. The only fundamental difference was that the Buddha achieved enlightenment through his own determination and as a result of long preparation, whereas his followers achieved it as a result of his teaching.

Someone who is considered to be enlightened in this way is termed an *arhat* (or *arahant* in Sanskrit). There are a number of titles given in the scriptures for different levels of spiritual achievement leading up to the level of arhat, for example, Stream Entrant (one who has entered the stream carrying a person on to Nibbana) or Once Returner (one who will be born once more before achieving Nibbana).

In some Mahayana scriptures, the title arahant is used for one who has achieved a personal spiritual status in a rather individualistic way, and it therefore contrasted with the Bodhisattva who is dedicated to the welfare of all. Although important for emphasizing the altruistic attitude of the bodhisattva, this is rather unfair on the arhats, since – although described conventionally as having achieved something as an individual – the whole essence of enlightenment is one that denies selfish individuality. A selfish arhat is therefore a contradiction in terms.

There may also be some confusion, because the Sanskrit term arahant was used widely of a spiritual teacher or guru in many of the Indian religious traditions. Whether those who achieved Buddhist enlightenment thought of themselves in terms of having gained some spiritual status is debatable, and certainly the idea of clinging on to such a status would be quite contrary to Buddhist teaching. On the other hand, the scriptures delight in celebrating the achievements of the Buddha's followers, and of using this to emphasize the success of his teaching.

see also...

Nibbana; Re-becoming

Avalokiteshvara

Of all the great Bodhisattvas, Avalokiteshvara is the most popular, especially in Tibetan Buddhism where he is known as 'Chenrezig'. The name means 'the lord who looks down (with compassion)'. Avalokiteshvara is therefore the embodiment of compassion, the one who hears the cries of those who suffer. In China, Avalokiteshvara becomes female in the persona of Kwan-shih-yin, known in Japan as Kannon.

Dedicated to saving people from suffering, Avalokiteshvara is said, in the Lotus Sutra, to take on 33 different forms in order to achieve his purpose. In part, this is reflected in the great variety of images used for him. Sometimes he is shown stepping down from a throne, expressing his willingness to enter into the world of suffering. A very popular image is the Avalokiteshvara with 1000 arms. These radiate out like the spokes of a wheel and express the idea of his presence, available to help everywhere and in every situation. He is often shown holding a lotus bud. This expresses the idea that he will help people to open, like the lotus, into Buddhahood. The same idea is expressed by images that show him with hands cupped together in the shape of a lotus bud.

As with many Mahayana images, it is usual for Avalokiteshvara to appear dressed as a prince, with elaborate headgear and garments. This, of course, is in stark contrast to the Theravadin images of Shakyamuni Buddha. Like many of the richer aspects of Mahayana worship, it aims to express the spiritual treasure and success of the Bodhisattva. Since he takes on many forms in order to show compassion, Tibetan Buddhists believe that he can be present to them in human form. The Dalai Lama is seen as an incarnation of this Bodhisattva – in other words, he is an embodiment of pure compassion. This has led to the popular misconception of the Dalai Lama as a 'god-king'.

see also...

Bodhisattva; Compassion; Dalai Lama; Lotus

Bardo States

There is often a difference between the philosophical ideas on which religion is based and their popular expression. The Buddhist teaching of 'no-self' (*anatta*) and re-becoming (*punabhava*), makes it clear that there is no independent or separate 'self' to pass from one life to the next, but that there is a stream of life within which the present influences the future. The life that follows this present one is not 'me' but is influenced by my life. As in the image of one flame lighting another, there are two separate flames but the second only arises because of the first.

Tibetan Buddhism, however, explores the *bardo* states – gaps between one thing and the next – of which the bardo of death is the most significant. Tibetans therefore anticipate an 'in-between' stage (the bardo) as a time of preparation for the next life, in which the individual, through various choices, influences his or her 'next' birth.

The Tibetan Book of the Dead is presented as an instruction manual for how to cross through the bardo state and enter into a rebirth. It is customary to read this to a person who is dying by way of comfort, and as a reminder that this life will influence another life yet to come. It sets out the experiences and choices that are to be made as one enters the bardo. Those attracted to a particular colour, for example, will tend to be born into the corresponding realm. There is even the moment of seeing a number of copulating couples, and feeling attracted to one particular person, male or female. That is seen as the moment when a person chooses their parents and, in a sense, witnesses their own conception. One's present inclinations and choices will therefore influence the future life.

As with all Buddhist teaching, it should not be taken in a crude or literal sense, but as a psychological exploration of the reality of facing death, and of recognizing the ongoing stream of life beyond it.

see also...

Death; Re-becoming; Tulkus

Bodhisattva

The literal translation of Bodhisattva is 'enlightenment being'. In the earliest tradition it describes one who is on the way to becoming a Buddha. So Siddhartha is called a Bodhisattva before his enlightenment, and the Jataka stories of 'the life that was to become the Buddha', show the career of a Bodhisattva.

The term took on a broader meaning in Mahayana Buddhism. A Bodhisattva is one who dedicates himself or herself to helping all beings to achieve peace and enlightenment, rather than seeking it in a selfish or individualistic way, and one becomes a Bodhisattva through the arising of the Bodhicitta (or Buddha mind).

At one level, all Buddhists may be seen as aspiring Bodhisattvas. The Bodhisattva vow is to help all creatures everywhere – and to defer one's own bliss of enlightenment until that is achieved. At another level, there developed a whole range of Bodhisattvas in the form of archetypal images, used in devotion, each describing a particular quality of enlightenment. Thus, Avalokiteshvara is the Bodhisattva of compassion and is sometimes shown with 1000 arms, each hand available to help creatures. At other times he is shown stepping down, coming to the aid of those who suffer. He is thought of as the one who hears the cries of the world. In Chinese Buddhism he changes sex and becomes Kwan-shih-yin. Manjushri is a bodhisattva associated with learning and is shown holding a book and wielding the sword of transcendental wisdom.

Mahayana shrines generally have many of these Bodhisattva images, often richly decorated and clothed as princes. These are not intended to represent the historical Buddha, Shakyamuni, but to celebrate spirutual qualities and as such are highly symbolic.

see also...

Avalokiteshvara

Brahma Viharas

When the Buddha first sent out his monks on their preaching tours, they were to go 'for the benefit and happiness of the many', in other words, their task was to promote the well being of all creatures. Yet, because Buddhism is presented as a system of personal training, aiming at wisdom and compassion, it might appear to be concerned mainly with the individual and his or her own development. This is true, but only in the sense that Buddhism sees personal transformation as a necessary first step. The result of this, however, should be seen in one's relationships with others, and this is described in terms of the four *Brahma Viharas*, or 'divine states' (literally, 'divine resting places'), the traditional qualities of the Buddhist attitude to life and other people.

The Brahma Viharas are *metta* (love), *karuna* (compassion), *mudita* (sympathetic joy) and *upekkha* (even-mindedness, or equanimity). They were set out by Buddhaghosa in the fifth century CE in his book *Visuddhimagga*, and show the essence of the Buddhist attitude towards others. By meditating on the Brahma Viharas, a Buddhist hopes to see people as they really are in themselves, not as they might appear to be, filtered through his or her own prejudices and needs.

Meditating upon and therefore cultivating the Brahma Viharas, allows the mind to settle gently into a positive attitude. It aims to allow a person to forgive himself or herself for their mistakes, accepting the imperfect reality of one's life on the basis of not being able to love and accept others unless you can first love and accept yourself. It also promotes a discerning but non-judgmental attitude towards others – seeing them without prejudice and entering into their situation, whether it be pain or pleasure, with genuine empathy, sharing joy or showing compassion as appropriate. The final one, equanimity, emphasizes the acceptance of both positive and negative aspects of reality without prejudice.

see also...

Compassion; Metta

Buddha

Buddha is not a name, but a title. It is used of someone who has achieved enlightenment (*bodhi*), and who is therefore fully awake to the truth of life. Most obviously, it is used of Sidhatta Gotama (Sanskrit: Siddhartha Gautama) the historical Buddha, who is often referred to as Shakyamuni, or 'Sage of the Shakyas'. However, it is only used of him after his enlightenment; prior to that, he is referred to as a Bodhisattva, or Buddha-to-be.

However, especially in the Mahayana tradition, the concept 'Buddha' has expanded considerably. First, it was believed that in each world system and age there would be a Buddha, whose purpose was to preach the Dhamma. Thus, in the Lotus Sutra – a key scripture for many Mahayana Buddhists – the connection is made between the historical Buddha and thousands of Buddha figures from other worlds, including those of endless ages in the past. In this sense, Buddha is used as a generic term for an enlightened teacher. This extension is important for Buddhist teaching, for it emphasizes that the teachings of the Buddha are not limited to any one historical period or situation, but are simply the particular expression of a universal truth.

Aspects of enlightenment may also be expressed through Buddha figures. Thus, for example, in the Mandala of the Five Buddhas, each represents a particular quality of enlightenment – imperturbability, generosity, meditative calm, mirror-like wisdom and teaching. Again, the images of the Buddhas – here perhaps the Buddha Amitabha (Amida) is probably the most instantly recognizable, sitting in calm meditation with hands folded in font of him – are representations of a universal reality. Through the idea of the Buddha nature, it is also recognized that Buddhahood is a possibility for every sentient being.

see also...

Buddha Nature; Enlightenment; Mandalas; Shakyamuni Buddha

Buddha Nature

By about the third century CE, some Buddhist teaching in India included the idea of the *Tathagatagarbha* or 'Buddha womb'. It proposed that beneath all the changing and interconnected elements that make up our lives, there is a level of reality in which the Buddha is within every being as its unchanging, permanent, non-conditioned nature. In other words, although you cannot see it through the clutter of life, deep within yourself, you (and all other creatures) are Buddha.

This should not be taken in any crude sense, because if there is a Buddha nature, it is beyond all conceptual thought. The Buddha nature is not something that can be examined or analyzed. It is not the result of rational analysis – for it is central to the whole Buddhist view of life that we cannot find an inner unchanging reality; we are simply a temporary putting together of the different strands (*skandhas*) of life. Rather, the idea of the Buddha nature is said to develop through meditation.

There are two ways of understanding Buddhist teaching (particularly in the Mahayana tradition). 'Transmission dhamma' is teaching that comes through the scriptures; 'realization dhamma' is teaching that comes as a result of the meditation and spiritual practice. The Buddha nature teaching belongs to this second tradition.

In the 'shentong' tradition of Tibetan Buddhism, emptiness (*shunyata*) implies a freedom from all faults and limitations, it is not 'nothing' but the reality that emerges once all illusions are cut away. This is the Buddha Wisdom Mind, or Buddha nature. However, it cannot be understood using our ordinary conceptualizing mind: it is beyond reason. It simply describes what is 'known' through meditation once the mind stops reasoning.

The Buddha nature refers to the natural ability all beings have to become Buddha. The fact that one is Buddha already does not mean that one should not strive on the path towards enlightenment – for your Buddha nature will only be revealed once illusions are pruned away.

see also...

Buddha; Shunyata; Trikaya doctrine

Chinese Buddhism

Buddhism arrived in China in the first and second century CE and gradually took root alongside the two existing religious philosophies, Taoism and Confucianism. The three influenced one another and were not generally regarded as mutually exclusive. Chinese Buddhism therefore inherited a culture that was very different from that of India.

The Pure Land School, based on reverence for Amida Buddha, established itself in the second century. The main practice of this tradition is calling on the name of Amida Buddha. This was promoted by the *Sukhavata Sutra* (Sukhavati meaning 'Pure Land') in about 350 CE. It teaches that no effort or discipline is needed in order to make spiritual progress, all that is required is to call upon the name of Amida Buddha, who will create a Buddha realm where conditions are ideal for the practice of the Dhamma. Kwan-shih-yin, the female Bodhisattva of compassion (seen as a female form of the very popular Bodhisattva Avalokiteshvara) became associated with Amida Buddha, and her images are frequently found on Chinese Buddhist shrines.

The other principle form of Buddhism to develop in China was Ch'an. This term (and its Japanese equivalent, Zen) means 'meditation'. It developed from the fifth and sixth centuries, promoted particularly by the figure of Bodhidharma, and by a succession of spiritual leaders known as the patriarchs. It divided into Northern and Southern schools, of which the Southern one survived. By 1000 CE it dominated all forms of Buddhism in China, apart from Pure Land.

Many features of Zen Buddhism in Japan originated in China, including the use of *kungan* (*koans* in Japanese) – enigmatic phrases, questions or short pieces of narrative, designed to block the normal process of rational analysis and to open the mind to sudden enlightenment. Hostile to all authority and intellectual formulations, Ch'an saw the primary purpose of spiritual practice as seeing into one's own true nature.

see also...

Koans; Mahayana Buddhism; Pure Land Buddhism; Zen

Chortens

In the Tibetan tradition, stupas (a monument enclosing the ashes or relics of the Buddha or one of his followers) are called chortens. Some of the symbolism of the chorten followed that of the earlier stupa tradition, but other elements were added. The design of a chorten (as with stupas generally) is symbolic, representing (in ascending order, starting at the base) the five elements: earth, water, fire, air and the pure ether or spirit. So, at one level the chorten represents the whole universe, but these same features also represent elements within the human person, with the physical body at the base (generally in the form of a cube, topped with a sphere or hemisphere). Above them, the cone and the inverted hemisphere represent the heart centre and the throat (speech) respectively. It is topped by a representation of pure spirit, corresponding to the enlightened mind. Thus, the chorten is a symbol of reality and of the path towards enlightenment.

On Tibetan chortens, at the base of the fire element (the cone, mid-way up the chorten), there may be a rectangular box called a *harmika*. This generally contains the relics of the person in whose memory the chorten has been built, but it may also be taken to represent an altar, upon which offerings would be sacrificed on a sacred fire. This symbolism clearly represents a very ancient tradition, since sacrifices of this sort are not found in Buddhism. Notice, however, that just as in non-Buddhist religion, a ritual sacrifice might be thought of as the point at which some spiritual gain is made, so in Buddhism, the harmika is located at the point at which the choices and decisions of the 'heart centre' start to lead upwards towards enlightenment. The harmika represents the moment of choice to enter onto the path of enlightenment. It is sometimes decorated with eyes. Chortens are further decorated with prayer flags, especially at festival times.

see also...

Stupas

Compassion

There are two qualities which characterize the Buddhist path: wisdom and compassion. The two are very closely linked. The starting point of Buddhist wisdom is the recognition that all things change, that everything is interconnected and that nothing in the world is ever going to give absolute or permanent satisfaction. This gives a sense of the unsatisfactoriness of life – *dukkha* (generally, if misleadingly, translated as 'suffering'). To recognize the 'emptiness' of individual things, to see their constant change and interconnectedness, is to become free from grasping and therefore to find happiness. Those who fail to see this reality in life are always tempted to grasp and hold on to things in a way that can only lead to more *dukkha*. Hence, wisdom is the key to lead us from unsatisfactoriness towards genuine happiness – those who see the suffering caused by ignorance and the greed and hatred that come from it, are led to seek to help sentient beings overcome it. In other words, they have an attitude of compassion towards the suffering of all living things.

Therefore, in Buddhism, compassion is not a moral requirement, but the natural response to its view of the nature of reality. When the Buddha sent out his disciples to teach, they were told to do so out of compassion for all creatures, for the welfare of gods and men. However, compassion is also expressed through the precepts (guidelines for the moral life) especially the first two: not to take life and not to steal.

Compassion is celebrated in many of the Jataka tales, which claim to be about former lives of the Buddha, in the compassion of a hunter who spares the life of a deer, for example, or of a hare who volunteers to give his own life to feed a starving man. Avalokiteshvara, along with the female images of Tara, and Kwan-shih-yin, is especially celebrated as the bodhisattva of compassion; and the whole concept of a Bodhisattva is of one who is dedicated to helping others.

see also...

Avalokiteshvara; Bodhisattva; Brahma Viharas; Jataka Tales

Conventional and Absolute Truth

Much of Buddhist philosophy is concerned with the analysis of what we experience; in other words, it tends to break down everything into its constituent parts. This has the effect of showing that complex things (like people) are not separate and permanent entities. Thus, on analysis, I recognize that my body is simply one small part of the physical stream of life, constantly being renewed by food, drink and oxygen. The aim of such analysis is to help people to overcome possessive craving and identification, by showing how everything changes and everything is interconnected.

The problem with this, however, is that in our ordinary lives we need to speak of complex things as though they were separate and permanent. I may know that I am comprised of five ever-changing *skandhas*, but I still have to introduce myself over the telephone as an individual who has sufficient permanence for the person on the other end of the line to recognize me!

In order to get over this problem, the distinction is sometimes made (particularly within Madhyamaka philosophy) between absolute truth and conventional truth. Although in an absolute sense, everything might be 'empty' (*shunya*), in ordinary conversation it is still important to speak of individual things as though they were separate entities. Thus, I have to speak of 'myself', although I may realize that there is no absolute or permanent thing that corresponds to that 'self'.

This does not suggest dishonesty. Modern science may teach us that a stone is, on analysis, merely a collection of atomic forces, but that does not stop me cautioning a child not to stumble over it. In the same way, Buddhist philosophy recognizes that something can be true in an absolute sense, but cannot be spoken of in that way all the time.

see also...

Philosophies; Shunyata; Skandhas

Craving (Tanha)

The Buddha taught that the fundamental cause of suffering is *tanha* or craving. It expresses an unhealthy attempt to grasp and find satisfaction in those things which, because they are constantly changing and insubstantial, are never actually going to be able to deliver true or permanent satisfaction. This is the second of the Four Noble Truths. It is the root cause of suffering and getting rid of tanha is therefore presented as the aim of the spiritual path and the way to happiness.

Tanha should not be mistaken for *chanda* (or 'desire') which can sometimes be a good thing. Thus, a desire for the Dhamma and enlightenment is a very positive quality. Notice that the attempt to eradicate craving is not at all the same as seeking to eliminate all pleasure in life. 'Don't hope for anything and you won't be disappointed' is a very poor caricature of what Buddhists actually believe. The very particular feature of tanha is that it attempts to appropriate its object, to hold on to it, and own it. It implies possessiveness as well as craving. Attempting to manipulate, possess and hold on to things is a hopeless task, for it goes against the fundamentally changing and insubstantial nature of reality. That is why it leads to suffering.

Craving can be for things mental as well as physical. There can be a craving for knowledge and certainty – the view that 'only this is true, everything else is false', or the desire to hold on to beliefs even after they have been shown to be false. The desire always to be in the right is particularly destructive. This is a form of intellectual craving and is as limiting and probably more damaging than the more obvious craving for material rewards or physical pleasure.

To celebrate and enjoy without grasping: that is the key to the Buddhist view of happiness.

see also...

Dukkha; Four Noble Truths

Dalai Lama

Within Tibetan Buddhism there are a number of different monastic orders, each with its own teaching lineages and traditions. The largest of these is the Gelugpa (meaning 'virtuous custom') commonly known as 'Yellow Hats', a reference to their ceremonial headgear. It was formed by Tsong-ka-pa in the fourteenth century as an attempt to reform the existing monastic order and to establish the vinaya rules that were used in Theravada monasteries.

The Grand Lama of Lhasa has traditionally been the head of the Gelugpa order, but from the sixteenth century he has also been known by the title Dalai Lama. The word 'dalai' means 'sea' and the title Dalai Lama therefore means 'the teacher who is profound or measureless (as the sea)'. In the seventeenth century, the fifth Dalai Lama became both religious and political leader of Tibet and built the Potala Palace at Lhasa. From then on, Dalai Lamas have taken on both a spiritual and political role and ruled Tibet until the mid-twentieth century.

Dalai Lamas (the present one is the fourteenth, each being a *tulku*, or reincarnation of the previous one) are thought of as an incarnation of Chenrezig (the Tibetan name for the Bodhisattva Avalokiteshvara) and thus an embodiment of compassion. It is this tradition that has led the Dalai Lama to be described in the West as the 'god-king' of Tibet. That, of course, makes little sense in Buddhist terms, since he certainly would not claim to be divine in any Western sense.

In 1959, nine years after the Chinese invasion of Tibet, and following an uprising in the country against the Chinese, the Dalai Lama escaped from Tibet and established himself in Dharamsala in northern India. He has become a focus for the community of Tibetan exiles and acts as a representative of the people and culture of Tibet as a whole, as well as being the spiritual head of the Tibetan people and of Tibetan Buddhists worldwide.

see also...

Avalokiteshvara; Tibetan Buddhism; Tulkus

Death

As popularly presented, Buddhists look forward to rebirth, following this life, depending upon the good or bad karma they have gathered. At this level, death is simply the reminder that a Buddhist should not seek happiness for this life only, but should see it in a much wider context, seeking through spiritual practice to achieve better lives in the future. At another level, however, this popular image is something of a caricature, since Buddhism does not teach the continuing existence of a 'self' or *atman* that can move from one life to another. Rather, life is seen as a process of constant change or re-becoming. Reflection on death is therefore a means of reminding oneself that all things in this life are impermanent and that one will die at some point in the future. Happiness that is grasped at and related to one's own life is therefore limited and may be a hindrance to seeing the wider stream of life of which one is a part.

In the Jataka tales about the Buddha's former lives, the characters are spoken of as 'the life that was to become the Buddha'. Buddhists may think of their present existence as being part of the stream of life that is to become something else in the future. Death is simply a point at which this stream flows on without one's present existence. In Tibetan Buddhism, there is believed to be a gap (or bardo) between one life and the next, the art of negotiating which is set out in *The Tibetan Book of the Dead.*

Buddhists are generally cremated. In the case of the Buddha and his chief followers, their cremated remains were distributed and enclosed within stupas, acting as memorials and places of pilgrimage and devotion. Today, the cremated remains of some Buddhists, particularly respected teachers, are set within permanent stupas. For others, their cremated remains may be placed in a small wooden stupa on a shrine.

see also...

Bardo States; Re-becoming

Dhamma (Dharma)

Dhamma, or Dharma as it is known in Sanskrit, has three different meanings, which should not be confused:

1 Dhamma can refer to the ultimate truth or reality of life – something that is beyond any verbal formula and is fully known by those who become enlightened.
2 It is also the term used for the teaching of the Buddha and his followers. It is therefore something preached and studied, and it is the second of the three Jewels to which Buddhists go for refuge.
3 Lastly, in Buddhist philosophy, as an exercise in breaking down the conventional way of seeing individual things, they may be reduced to their component parts in experience – to the simple elements of which they are composed. These, too, are termed 'dhammas' and, in early Buddhist teaching, they continued in existence, coming together on a temporary basis in order to form complex beings and then separating out again. They can therefore perhaps be thought of as the atoms and molecules out of which everything is formed.

There is actually a fourth but less common use of this term. One can speak of mastering various 'dhammas', meaning skills or specific areas of knowledge.

Using it in its principal way – namely as the teaching of the Buddha – it is important to remember that the Dhamma is not simply to be identified with a particular form of words or formula, however central to the Buddhist understanding of life (for example, the Noble Eightfold Path or the Four Noble Truths). These are one way in which Dhamma is expressed, and they may be learned and reflected on in order to achieve wisdom – but they are not ultimately to be identified as the whole of the Dhamma, which may take many forms according to the needs of those to whom it is addressed. All Buddhist teaching is aimed at personal reflection and application, none is accepted simply on the basis of speculation.

see also...

Dhammachakra; Eightfold Path; Four Noble Truths; Interconnectedness

Dhammachakra

Following his enlightenment and the decision that he should teach the Dhamma, the Buddha is said to have gone in search of the five ascetics with whom he had practised and who had deserted him when he gave up his extreme ascetic practices. He is described as meeting them in the Deer Park at Sarnath (then called Isipatana) near Benares, and of so impressing them by his appearance that they could not ignore him (as they had intended), but are described as accepting him and receiving from him his first 'sermon', which is traditionally termed 'the first turning of the wheel of the Dhamma', and is set out in the Sutra of that name, the *Dhammacakkapavattana-sutta*. Dhammachakra, therefore, means 'wheel of the Dhamma', and finds its origin in that first teaching.

There is a dhammachakra mudra which shows the Buddha with his hands held in front of his chest, with his fingers positioned as though turning a small wheel, and this, of course, is the traditional image for his teaching.

In a traditional Buddhist formula, the *Ti Ratana Vandana*, the Dhamma is described as 'immediately apparent, always coming to life, taking the form of a personal invitation, progressive, and to be understood individually by those who are wise.' This is crucial for understanding Buddhist Dhamma: it is not a set of propositions to be accepted or rejected. Rather, it is a process which is personal and individual, leading to insights that become apparent to different people in different ways. It is the invitation to an ongoing process of examination, not the end product of a ready-digested system of thought.

The Mahayana and Vajrayana may be thought of as subsequent turnings of the dhammachakra, as distinct but related parts of an ongoing movement.

see also...

Dhamma; Shakyamuni Buddha

Dhammapada

The *Dhammapada* ('path' or 'way' of the Teaching) is probably the best known of all portions of Buddhist scripture. It comes from the Sutta Pitaka, part of the early Pali Canon, and is thus accepted by all branches of Buddhism. It is a collection of the teachings of the Buddha, in which various short passages have been arranged into themes. The opening section of the Dhammapada expresses some of the key themes in Buddhist teaching:

> What we are today comes from our thoughts of yesterday, and our present thoughts build our life of tomorrow: our life is the creation of our mind. If a man speaks or acts with an impure mind, suffering follows him as the wheel of the cart follows the beast that draws the cart.
> … If a man speaks or acts with a pure mind, joy follows him as his own shadow.
>
> Hate is not conquered by hate: hate is conquered by love. This is the law eternal. Many do not know that we are here in this world to live in harmony. Those who know this do not fight against one another.
>
> If a man speaks many holy words but he speaks and does not [act on them], this thoughtless man cannot enjoy the life of holiness; he is like a cowherd who counts the cows of his master. Whereas if a man speaks but a few holy words and yet he lives the life of those words, free from passion and hate and illusion – with right vision and a mind free, craving for nothing both now and hereafter – the life of this man is a life of holiness.

As these examples show, the Dhammapada is quite unlike the more usual dialogue form found in Buddhist scriptures. In style (and partly in content) it is sometimes compared with the Sermon on the Mount in the Christian tradition.

see also...

Scriptures; Sutras

Dhyana States

The important thing about Buddhist meditation is not the actual experience that a person has when sitting, but the effect that meditation has on their habitual way of looking at the world. In other words, meditation is essentially a means to an end, and not an end in itself. On the other hand, there are various stages in the process of meditation as a person becomes more and more calm and integrated. These are known as the *dhyanas*, or stages of meditative absorption. They are traditionally described in terms of images:

1 Of the mixing of soap powder and water in a ball, blending it until the whole of the ball is saturated with water. So, the peace of the first dhyana pervades the whole body, leaving the meditator calm and integrated.

2 Like a pool of water fed by an underground spring, constantly being refreshed by water welling up from below, a stage describing the inflowing of new insights and creativity. In Western terms it could be described as the stage at which one is particularly open to the unconscious.

3 Like a lake full of lotuses, some growing up through the water, some breaking the surface and opening out. The water pervades everything.

4 Like a person who has bathed, sitting, covered round with a white sheet. One is wrapped about by the mediation, protected and clear.

These are just the dhyanas of form, but there are also lists of formless dhyanas, the result of analysis of the progressively more refined levels of consciousness achieved through meditation. The achievement of the dhyanas is not an end in itself, but they do represent moments when the mental hindrances are suspended and give a taste of what is spiritually possible.

see also...

Meditation

Diversity

There is remarkable diversity within Buddhism. First, there are the three major 'vehicles': the Hinayana, Mahayana and Vajrayana. Within each of these there is variety – between monastic life and the practices of lay Buddhists, for example, or between different forms of the Mahayana. It is difficult, on the surface, to see what the simplicity of Zen and the richness of Tibetan worship have in common. Equally, in terms of images, one has tremendous diversity, from the absolute plainness of a Zendo, and the simple images of some Theravada Buddhas, through to the elaborate princely figures of Tibetan Buddhas and Bodhisattvas. Some Buddhists chant, most meditate, some take part in puja (worship) regularly, others very seldom.

This diversity has come about principally because Buddhist teaching encourages critical examination. From the earliest days, there was diversity within the community of monks. Yet in general, this did not lead to animosity, or declaring some orthodox and others heretics (which tends to happen in religions which have set forms of belief to which all followers are required to subscribe). Rather, different traditions grew up alongside one another, sometimes becoming separated through geographical movement.

The other reason for the diversity is the general Buddhist principle that teachings are to be adapted to the needs of those being taught. Different cultural and social conditions suggest different approaches to, and emphases within, Buddhist dhamma (teaching). Thus, for example, in China, where there had been a long history of family loyalty as a sign of piety, Buddhism tended to emphasize the role of the laity and family life, whereas in India, where there had been a long tradition of individual monasticism and asceticism, is was natural for the Buddhist community to be focused on the monastic, celibate life as it had done from the start.

Generally speaking, practitioners of the different forms of Buddhism are very tolerant of one another.

see also...

Chinese Buddhism; Hinayana; Japanese Buddhism; Mahayana; Tibetan Buddhism; Vajrayana

Dukkha

Since we live in a world where everything is temporary, liable to change and interconnected, nothing can satisfy us completely and permanently. This is the basic fact of life from which the Buddhist quest starts, and it is referred to as *dukkha*. Dukkha is often translated as meaning 'suffering', but it means something more like 'unsatisfactoriness', a sense that life never quite lives up to our expectations, or realizing that even enjoyable things cannot last for ever.

One aspect of dukkha is given in the traditional lists of things that cause suffering: lust, craving, greed, attachment, grasping, hatred and aversion. These are all mental attitudes towards the world. The achievement of *nibbana* (*nirvana*) is the point at which the fires of greed, hatred and ignorance go out for lack of fuel. Of course, ignorance (not seeing the interconnectedness of things) leads to attachment and grasping.

The key to the Buddhist vision of overcoming dukkha, is not that one should somehow be removed from the realities of life (after all, the Buddha himself suffered and died), but to have an attitude of non-attachment that allows one to cope with the limitations of life in a way that does not lead to further suffering. It is a matter of removing those psychological tendencies (clinging to things that inevitably change; craving things that cannot give satisfaction) that bring additional, existential suffering when faced with the natural limitations of life.

Buddhist teaching is not negative. It starts with the recognition of the inevitability of dukkha, but does so only in the context of setting out a path to overcome it.

see also...

Four Noble Truths; Samsara

Eightfold Path

The Noble Eightfold Path is a summary of the Buddhist philosophy and practice. Each step in the path expresses an element in Buddhist life and teaching, so they are designed to be taken together, not in the order in which they appear.

The first two deal with wisdom:

1 Right (or perfect) Understanding (in other words, a basic awareness of the Buddhist view of reality, without which there is no insight or reason to follow the path).

2 Right Emotion (knowledge needs to be linked to personal conviction and intention, if any progress is to be made).

The next three deal with ethics, in the broad sense:

3 Right Speech (this appears as the fourth of the precepts).

4 Right Action (summed up in the five precepts).

5 Right Livelihood (in order that one's work is in line with the precepts).

The final three deal with mental training:

6 Right Effort (the cultivation and maintaining of positive emotions and thoughts, the elimination and prevention of negative emotions and thoughts – this is seen as a constant process of being aware of mental states and taking action to influence them).

7 Right Mindfulness (a key feature of Buddhist mental training).

8 Right Contemplation (or meditation).

The threefold division of these eight steps is sometimes used to describe Buddhism as 'the triple way' of *prajna* (wisdom), *sila* (morality) and *samadhi* (meditation).

Lists are a feature of Buddhist teaching. They are used as an aid to the systematic exposition and remembering of the Dhamma and help to get its various elements in balance. It is important to recognize, however, that they are not meant to be exclusive. One can speak of the eightfold path, the triple way, the six paramitars – all of which will outline essential features of Buddhist teaching.

see also...

Dhamma; Meditation; Mindfulness; Precepts

Enlightenment

The Buddha was said to have achieved enlightenment as he sat beneath the Bo tree. This is, in broad terms, a state of full knowledge of things as they really are, including an awareness of former lives and how things come into being and pass out of being. It is not presented in conceptual terms (there is no formula for enlightenment) since it is rather a state in which a person has full awareness – a way of seeing, rather than simply the content of what is seen.

The experience of enlightenment was not limited to the Buddha himself, since his followers were also described as having achieved this state. The significant difference is that the Buddha achieved the state unaided, whilst his followers achieved it with the benefit of his teachings.

The term most closely associated with enlightenment is *nibbana* (or *nirvana*), meaning a state in which there is no more fuel for the triple fires of greed, hatred and delusion. Such a state brings in new peace, happiness and insight and may lead to enlightenment.

In the Zen tradition, the process of becoming enlightened is by way of spontaneous flashes of insight, termed *satori*.

One of the key features of enlightenment is that it is the recognition of a spiritual state that has been achieved – it is not a 'thing' to receive, but the acknowledgement of a way of seeing and responding to life. It is believed that the Buddha prepared for his enlightenment (and his Buddhahood) over many lifetimes. Therefore, ordinary Buddhists do not expect to achieve enlightenment within this life, simply to move in that direction.

see also...

Buddha; Nibbana

Festivals

Each of the three main branches of Buddhism has its festivals. For Theravadins (and shared throughout the Buddhist world) the most important festival is Wesak, which commemorates the Buddha's birth, enlightenment and death. It is celebrated on the day of the full moon in April/May. Lay people may take on extra precepts for the day, by way of voluntary spiritual discipline, and the day is generally spent listening to talks and taking part in devotional worship. The symbol of light features widely, with lamps placed in windows or carried in procession.

July sees the celebration of the Buddha's first sermon, and in October, as the end of the rains retreat, there is a Theravadin ceremony called Kathina, in which lay people provide robes and other necessities for the monks. In Burma and Thailand, New Year is celebrated in the spring, and is particularly associated with freedom – by releasing fish or eels into fresh water, or releasing birds from cages. Buddha images may be washed and garlanded, and children splash water over one another, representing the cleansing of a new start.

Mahayana Buddhists have their own distinctive festivals. O-bon, held in July, is the festival of 'the hungry ghosts' when people remember those who have died and make offerings, thereby traditionally feeding those who (through their meanness in this life) are in the world of hungry spirits, as described on the Wheel of Life.

Among the colourful Tibetan festivals, the New Year is celebrated in the spring with games, dance-dramas and the construction of large butter sculptures.

In Japan the Buddha's birthday is celebrated on 8 April and his death on 19 February. Some Zen circles in the West have changed the traditional dates of Buddhist festivals in order to fit in with Western social festivals. For example, celebrating the Buddha's enlightenment on 25 December (Christmas) rather than 8 December, the traditional date for this in Japan.

see also...

Wesak; Wheel of Life

Fetters, The Ten

Ordinary, unenlightened people are said to be bound by ten fetters. They are:

1. Personality view. In other words, seeing oneself as an independent entity with a fixed notion of 'self'. As long as this basic view persists, it is difficult to progress towards the overcoming of craving and suffering, simply because there is a fundamental division between 'the world' and 'myself', a division which serves only to highlight the temporary and vulnerable nature of this apparently separate 'self'.
2. Sceptical doubt. Buddhism does not require beliefs to be taken on trust, but only an openness and willingness to learn, which an over-critical attitude might prevent.
3. Reliance on ethical rules and religious observances. Whilst Buddhism certainly encourages ethical awareness and does not dismiss religious ceremonies, it holds that they are of benefit only in terms of the mental state of those who perform them. There is no inherent value in obedience as such, nor should religious rites be taken as a guaranteed method of making spiritual progress.
4. Craving for things of the senses. As in the centre of the Wheel of Life, greed or craving, along with hatred, feed (and are fed by) ignorance, and together these prevent a person from seeing things as they really are.
5. Hatred.
6. Craving for the world of archetypal forms. This, and the following fetter, refers to states of awareness achieved in meditation, to which one might be tempted to cling.
7. Craving for the formless world.
8. Conceit.
9. Restlessness.
10. Ignorance.

Traditionally it is believed that the person who is able to break the first three fetters achieves 'Stream Entry' – in other words, enters a stream which is bound to carry him or her to Nibbana. One who can break all ten fetters achieves enlightenment (i.e. becomes an arhat).

see also...

Anatta; Craving; Morality; Nibbana

Four Noble Truths

This is an early and basic way of setting out the teaching of the Buddha, under four headings: *dukkha* (suffering), *tanha* (craving), *niroda* (cessation) and *magga* (path).

1. **1** Dukkha, or unsatisfactoriness, is the recognition that life will involve change and decay, loss and frustration, simply because nothing is permanent.
2. **2** The cause of unsatisfactoriness is craving (tanha), the attempt to hold onto what cannot be held, to long to become permanent or even to want annihilation. In other words, the false longing for things either to be permanent and ultimately satisfying, or else to let them vanish entirely. In the real world, neither is possible, for everything interconnects.
3. **3** Cessation (niroda) of craving leads to a cessation of suffering, in other words to Nibbana (Nirvana) – the point at which the craving in greed, hatred and ignorance are replaced by generosity, love and insight.
4. **4** The path leading to Nibbana is the Noble Eightfold Path.

Together these truths show the intention of the Buddhist teaching, since they are set out in the way that is parallel with a traditional medical diagnosis and treatment. The illness is dukkha and its cause is tanha. Cure is possible (niroda) and the action to be taken in order to secure that cure is magga.

Since it starts with the recognition of suffering as a basic feature of life, this formulation of Buddhist teaching may give the impression that Buddhism is essentially pessimistic about life. However, the First Noble Truth does not affirm suffering as a necessary feature of life, but only as an experienced fact, which people seek to overcome. Its intention, as is shown in the other Noble Truths, is entirely positive in offering a cure for suffering.

see also...

Dhamma; Eightfold Path; Nibbana

Four Sights

According to the traditions about the life of Siddhartha Gautama prior to his enlightenment, his father tried to shield him from exposure to the harsh realities of life, hoping to prevent Siddhartha from encountering those things that might lead him to become religious, and encouraging him to continue in the lifestyle of a local ruler. However, Siddhartha is described as going out of his palace in his chariot, accompanied by his charioteer, Channa, and seeing four sights: an old man, a sick man, a corpse and a *sadhu* (holy man).

After each of the first three, Siddhartha recognized that everyone grows old, that everyone is liable to sickness and that everyone will eventually die. These things were said to have affected him deeply, and to have made him dissatisfied with his life of luxury, simply because he recognized that his wealth could not shield him from the universal nature of the human condition. To use the term that was to become the starting point in setting out the Buddha's teaching – he recognized the universal and inescapable nature of *dukkha*.

The fourth sight (the sadhu) introduced him to the concept of the religious quest as a way of understanding life and overcoming suffering. At the time, there were two very different religious traditions in Northern India. On the one hand there was the ritualized and formal religion of the Brahmins, and on the other there was a large number of itinerant religious ascetics and teachers, expounding a variety of philosophies and practices. Siddhartha's encounter with the sadhu suggested to him a way of seeking answers to his dilemma about the unsatisfactoriness of life.

The actual circumstances of Siddhartha's encounter with these four things is largely irrelevant. What we have now is a narrative which sets out in graphic and personal terms the reason for the religious quest that led eventually to enlightenment.

see also...

Dukkha; Shakyamuni Buddha

Hinayana

There is, and has always been, a variety of philosophies and practices within the Buddhist community. The three broadly based traditions are the Hinayana (small vehicle), along with the Mahayana (great vehicle), found especially in the Far East; and Vajrayana (diamond vehicle) found particularly in Tibet and the Tibetan communities worldwide. All three traditions are found in the West.

The early Hinayana traditions are represented today by the Theravada, found particularly in India, Sri Lanka, and South East Asia. The term Hinayana is a rather unfortunate and possibly misleading one. It means 'small vehicle' and was used in contrast to the Mahayana, or 'great vehicle'. The principal difference being that the former placed emphasis on personal effort towards Nibbana, with the goal of becoming arhat, whereas the latter emphasized universal Buddhahood and the ideal of the Bodhisattva, who is devoted to bringing all living creatures to enlightenment. The Mahayana also portrayed itself as being equally suited to monastic and lay Buddhists, whereas the Hinayana placed greater emphasis on the monastic life.

However, it would be a caricature to suggest that the Hinayana is selfish or narrow. This early tradition was (like all Buddhism) concerned to get away from the idea of the separate self or ego. Even where personal effort or the monastic ideal is emphasized, it aims at promoting *metta* (loving kindness) and compassion towards all.

Notice how many Buddhist terms include the idea of movement or journeying. The three branches of Buddhism are termed *yanas* (vehicles), and the Dhamma itself is called a Middle Way. You have the Eightfold Path, and the teaching is the turning of a wheel. Even the basic terms for suffering and happiness (*dukkha* and *sukha*) may have their origins in bad- and well-fitting chariot wheels; contrasting experiences on the journey through life.

see also...

Arhats; Diversity; Theravada

Images

The images of Buddhas and Bodhisattvas are called 'rupas', and they are found on shrines as a focal point for devotion. Offerings are made before them and they may be garlanded or washed during festivals as a mark of respect. However, they are not treated as being inherently holy, for that would go against the fundamental Buddhist philosophy. Some images (particularly those found in the Theravada) are very simple and represent the historical Buddha, Shakyamuni. He may be shown standing, sitting or lying on his side, and with a variety of hand positions (*mudras*), each of which has symbolic meaning. Traditionally, there are 32 characteristics of a Buddha and some of these, for example long ear lobes, are found on most images.

There are a great variety of Buddha images within Mahayana and Vajrayana Buddhism. The most widely recognized is that of Amida (Amitabha), of oriental appearance and sitting in deep meditation, legs crossed and hands together in front of the body in the meditation *mudra*. There are also female Buddha images, particularly Tara (in both white and green forms) and Kwan-shih-yin, both expressing compassion.

Bodhisattvas are often shown as princes, dressed elaborately with head-dresses. Colour, gesture and posture all convey symbolic meaning. In the case of Avalokiteshvara, stepping down from his throne, or having 1000 arms radiating out in all directions, both indicate that he is ever present to help those who suffer. Manjushri, representing learning and success, brandishes a sword of transcendental wisdom in one hand and holds a book of scriptures in the other.

For several hundred years, following the death of the Buddha, there were no images of him. Buddhist devotion focused on *stupas* (monuments containing his remains, or those of one of his followers) and the Buddha himself was represented by the eight-spoked wheel, or the stylized Buddha footprint.

see also...

Amitabha; Avalokiteshvara; Bodhisattva; Mudras; Shrines; Stupas

Impermanence (Anicca)

Anicca is one of the three Marks of Existence. In other words, one of the three features of existence upon which the entire Buddhist philosophy is based. It expresses the idea that everything that comes into existence will at some time also cease to exist; that everything is impermanent. This follows on from the basic view that things come about through causes and conditions (*paticcasamupada*). Things are maintained in their existence through many causes external to themselves, and as those causes change, so they too will change.

As with all Buddhist ideas, this is not merely speculation about the nature of existence (although, as such, it is in line with modern science) but has moral and spiritual elements as well. The key feature here is the tendency people have to grasp at things, hoping that they will not change or die, and that they will be a permanent source of comfort or pleasure. Such grasping can be towards another person, a career, wealth, status or even an idea or belief. Anicca, is the radical reminder that all such grasping is unsatisfactory, because the desired object, however good in itself, is also impermanent.

The same is true of experiences, feelings and ideas. The practice of mindfulness is one in which each separate mental experience is acknowledged and then set aside – a basic awareness that our experience is a constant flow of changing ideas and emotions.

Anicca is not seen as negative (although is experienced as such by those who continue to crave and grasp at permanence), but as a positive quality, since it allows change and growth. As part of a continuing stream of mental and physical energy, each particular thing or person is part of a natural process, and its fulfilment and happiness is found in that flow, not in isolation.

see also...

Interconnectedness; Marks of Existence; Samsara

Interconnectedness

This is the key term for understanding Buddhist philosophy; everything else depends upon it. The Pali term is *paticcasamupada* (Sanskrit: *pratityasamutpada*), and common translations for this are 'conditioned co-production' and 'dependent origination'. It means 'stepping up together', and it expresses a fundamental interconnectedness of all things. Whatever happens, happens as a result of causes and conditions. In its simplest form it says: 'This being so, that arises. This ceasing, that ceases.'

There are two ways of approaching this. First, it is a basic view of the way in which everything comes about – a view that is very close to that of modern science. Everything is able to be what it is, because of causes and conditions that radiate outwards to include the way the whole universe is structured. Second, all Buddhist teaching relates in some way to ethics and practice, so interconnectedness has further significance: through kamma (karma), our consciously chosen actions have consequences.

Paticcasamupada represents a middle way between two extreme philosophical positions. On the one hand, eternalism (where everything has its fixed nature) and nihilism (where nothing has any continuity or value). Things do exist, do have value, do make a difference – but only within the overall flow of existence. Whatever exists, is maintained in that existence by innumerable causes and conditions. We may think of human beings as existing over against the rest of nature, but deprived of oxygen, food or water they cease to exist almost immediately. Life on this planet depends on many factors, including the size of the Earth, its distance from the sun, the age of the sun etc. One day those conditions will change, and the Earth will disappear. At one time (prior to about five billion years ago) conditions were only just bringing our sun and planets into existence. Everything flows on and changes – the key feature of Buddhist wisdom.

see also...

Dhamma; Kamma; Middle Way

Japanese Buddhism

Buddhism arrived in Japan from Korea and China in the middle of the sixth century CE and was formally accepted by the ruler, Shotoku Taishi (593–622 CE), who promoted it as the official religion. Over the centuries that followed a number of different forms of Mahayana Buddhism became established and divided into distinct groupings, so that today there are over 100 different Buddhist sects in Japan. In the eighth century, Tendai Buddhism, which combined meditation with ritual and ceremonial, was introduced by a nobleman called Saicho, later known as Dengyo Daishi. Shingon, which included Tantric practices, similar to those in Tibetan Buddhism, was established by Kukai.

The twelfth and thirteenth centuries saw two distinct forms of Pure Land Buddhism: Honen established *Jodo*, and a little later Shinran Shonin founded *Jodo Shin-shu*. As all Pure Land groups, practice is focused on meditation, and it is believed that those who call on the name of Amida Buddha will be transported at death to a paradise where conditions for spiritual progress will be ideal.

Nichiren Buddhism, related to the Pure Land tradition, was founded by Nichiren (thirteenth century), and was politically aware and nationalistic. Sokka Gakkai, a worldwide lay Buddhist movement, is a modern branch of Nichiren Buddhism.

Zen is the Japanese term for meditation, and this form of Buddhism came to Japan from China, becoming established in the twelfth century. The two main groups are Rinzai, with special emphasis on sudden enlightenment (moments of *satori*) and the use of koans, and Soto, which emphasized a more gradual and traditional spiritual practice based on sitting meditation.

Buddhism has had a profound influence on Japanese art and culture and in turn has found itself adapting to its surroundings. In particular, Buddhist groups in Japan have tended to blur the traditional distinction between the monastic and the lay life.

see also...

Diversity; Nichiren; Pure Land Buddhism; Zen

Jataka Tales

The Jatakas are a collection of 547 stories, which illustrate qualities such as loyalty, compassion, self-sacrifice and insight. Many are introduced as being about 'the life that was to become the Buddha.' In other words, they claim to illustrate those actions and qualities that, through successive lives, prepared the way for the birth of the Buddha. They are often introduced by the account of a discussion between the Buddha and his followers about a particular action or moral quality.

Some stories feature animals, and the same animal may illustrate different qualities in different stories. For example, in one story a jackal tries to attack an elephant and is crushed, while a lion looks on. At the end of the story, the lion is identified with the Buddha and the jackal with Devadatta, who is said to have attempted to kill the Buddha in order to take control of the Order. In this case, the story illustrates the folly of attempting something beyond your powers. However, another story has a jackal rescuing a lion who is stuck fast in the mud, and then being befriended by him. Here, the lion is again identified with Buddha and the jackal with his cousin and companion Ananda.

There are elements of magic in many of the stories and of people receiving the just rewards (good or bad) of their action. When a stag is caught in a trap, the doe pleads with the approaching hunter to release it, and for her to be allowed to die alongside her mate. The hunter spares them both and the stag gives him a magic jewel as his reward. They illustrate (in a simplistic way) the principle of kamma (karma): that actions have consequences.

The Jatakas are a delightful teaching aid – illustrating many aspects of Buddhist wisdom and ethics, in a way that is emotionally engaging.

see also...

Bodhisattva; Morality; Shakyamuni Buddha

Kamma (Karma)

At its simplest, the Buddhist idea of *kamma* may be expressed as 'actions have consequences'. This does not imply that one's present situation is determined entirely by one's past actions, for that would deny the possibility of change and is contrary to Buddhist teaching. The principle of kamma is that unwholesome tendencies (*kilesa*) lead to actions (kamma) which produce fruits or results (*vipaka*). This is part – but only part – of the ongoing process of change described as Dependent Origination, one's past actions are therefore only one factor in the present equation, but a significant factor, because your past influences how you experience your present.

The Buddha taught that there were three errors concerning the causes of happiness or suffering:

1 that they were entirely related to past kamma
2 that they were the will of the gods
3 that they were uncontrollable, determined by luck or fate.

The present effects of negative actions performed in the past will depend on the qualities of the individual. The Buddha used the image of putting a chunk of salt into a small vessel of water and into a river. In the one, the water becomes very salty, in the other it makes little difference. Therefore the same action will have different degrees of significance for different people. Past action is a factor in sensation (*vedana*); in other words, how you experience things now depends in part on your past actions and experiences. That follows from the overall sense of a flow of existence, in which everything is capable of change, but nothing is completely lost. Every action contributes, but the results of that contribution depend on many other factors.

Whilst accepting responsibility for past actions and their consequences, and recognizing the way in which these shape one's present experience, the principle of kamma allows present choices to counter any negative effects from one's past. Buddhism does not treat it as in any way fatalistic.

see also...

Interconnectedness; Twelve Links; Wheel of Life

Koans

In Ch'an (Zen) Buddhism, a person is encouraged to get beyond conventional logic and analysis, and to achieve a direct perception of the nature of reality. However, in order to achieve this, it is necessary to break from the more usual methods of thinking and reasoning. One way of achieving this is by the use of *koans*. A koan is a short puzzle or riddle that makes no sense, or to which there is no answer, in terms of ordinary logic. The idea is that in trying to understand it, the mind batters itself against the koan until it is forced to go beyond ordinary logic. There is still no 'answer' to the koan, but suddenly something is seen that gets beyond it.

There are some very well-known koans, including, for example; 'What is the sound of one hand clapping?' Time and time again, you are thrown back on yourself, for example; 'Ask about Buddha, you will only get your own name as answer.'

If you think you have the answer to a koan, it probably means that you have misunderstood it. A koan is not a cryptic way of presenting an obvious truth, but a way of tricking the mind into looking at things differently.

Collections of koans were developed and used in particular monasteries, often with introductions and commentaries added at a later date. Together they form a tradition of mental training. One such collection is known as the Blue Cliff Record, named after the monastery in China where it was written down. This collection was brought to Japan by Dogen, when he returned from China to establish Soto Zen. It is sometimes said that koans are used mainly within the Rinzai Zen tradition, in contrast to the slow process of meditation favoured by Soto Zen, but this is not strictly true, for Soto Zen has also used koans since the time of its founding by Dogen.

see also...

Zen

Lotus

There is a story in the Buddhist scriptures that, shortly after his enlightenment, the Buddha remained at Bodh Gaya meditating, unsure about whether people would understand if he were to preach his new knowledge. He was approached by Brahma Sahampati, chief of the Hindu gods, who requested that he go and preach, saying that people were like lotuses in a lake. Some were still growing up through the water, others had reached the surface, and some were clear of the water and ready to open out and blossom. Thus, there would be at least some people who were ready to hear and respond to the Buddha's teaching. The lotus has therefore become a symbol of the mind on its path to enlightenment, capable of opening out into a 'thousand petalled lotus'.

The lotus appears throughout Buddhist iconography. Some images of Buddhas and Bodhisattvas show them sitting on a lotus throne, as though emerging from its petals, or holding a lotus. In general, any image containing a lotus indicates that what is being shown is spiritual or transcendent, rather than being a representation of something that exists in a mundane, physical sense.

Avalokiteshvara, the Bodhisattva of Compassion, is known as 'The Jewel in the Lotus', and the Lotus Sutra is the most popular and revered of all the Mahayana scriptures. Amitabha (Amida), the Buddha who represents loving compassion, has the lotus flower as his symbol. Sometimes, when taking part in worship, Buddhists may cup their hands, finger tips and thumbs together, pointing away from the body. This looks rather like the usual 'hands together' tradition of prayer or paying respect, but the hands are held apart, making the shape of a lotus bud. The 'jewel' contained within that lotus bud is, of course, the enlightened mind.

see also...

Amitabha; Avalokiteshvara; Images; Lotus Sutra; Shakyamuni Buddha

Lotus Sutra

The Lotus Sutra is the most influential of all the Mahayana scriptures, and is quite different in character from the early sutras. It opens with the Buddha preparing to speak to a gathering of thousands of followers. Eighty thousand Bodhisattvas are said to make offerings to hundreds of thousands of Buddhas in innumerable world systems. During this sutra, the historical Buddha is identified with countless Buddha figures: in other words, he represents a universal Buddha principle.

A key teaching is that, in the past, the Buddha taught three ways to salvation; one leading individuals to become Arhats; one leading them to become Pratyekabuddhas, enlightened for their own benefit; and one leading to the ideal of the Bodhisattva, enlightened for the sake of all. Now, however, these are to be superseded by a single goal: Buddhahood. At a crucial point in the fifteenth chapter of the sutra, the earth opens up and a vast number of Bodhisattvas rise up out of it. They are numerous as the sands of 60,000 Ganges Rivers, each with an equally huge retinue. This rich visual tapestry seeks to inspire the reader to see Buddhahood as both attainable by all, and also as a unifying truth throughout time and space. In each of innumerable world systems there are Buddhas teaching, and they all give essentially the same message.

Using many wonderful images, the Lotus Sutra therefore expands the vision of what Buddhism is about. Curiously, however, although there are many references to the Buddha being about to preach, or having preached the Lotus Sutra and the response of the vast company to hearing it, there is no section giving the teaching itself. In other words, the Lotus Sutra is about the preaching of the Lotus Sutra – its new teaching itself is not given directly. Some Mahayana Buddhists explain this in terms of the teaching being beyond words and concepts; as something that can be discovered only through devotion.

see also...

Mahayana; Nichiren

Mahayana

There are three branches or 'vehicles' within Buddhism. The earliest (represented now by the Theravada) was termed the Hinayana (small vehicle) on account of its emphasis on the individual quest for enlightenment. From this developed the Mahayana (large vehicle), with a spirituality based on universal altruism, found mainly in the Far East. Finally there was the Vajrayana (diamond vehicle) emphasizing ritual and devotional practices, and found today within the Tibetan tradition. These were not successive phases in Buddhist development, but developed alongside one another in India during the first millennium CE.

There had always been variety of practice and teaching within the early Sangha. By the fourth century BCE, one group – the Mahasanghikas – already had ideas of transcendental Buddhas which parallel later developments. It is generally held that the Mahayana was a development within some Buddhist communities that took place informally between 100 BCE and about 150 CE, and after that developed particular schools of teaching of its own – Madhyamaka and Yogacara.

Distinctive features of the Mahayana included:

- its emphasis on compassion and wisdom as the way of salvation
- the ideal of the Arhat, or individual enlightened person, was replaced by the Bodhisattva, who delays personal enlightenment in order to promote enlightenment for all
- the cultivation of the six paramitars, as ideals of the moral and spiritual life
- the use of a range of images of Buddhas and Bodhisattvas in worship
- the shift in emphasis from obedience to precepts and rules to accepting the idea that actions are seen as skilful or unskilful.
- the development of the idea of Shunyata (emptiness) as a way of expressing the radical nature of Anatta, that things do not have an inherent or permanent essence.

see also...

Chinese Buddhism; Diversity; Japanese Buddhism

Mandalas

Particularly in Tibetan Buddhism, there is a tradition of making intricate patterns, set within a circle (which is the literal meaning of the Sanskrit word *mandala*), often showing features of Buddhas and Bodhisattvas. These are sometimes painted but are often composed of grains of very fine coloured sand. They 'pattern out' and relate aspects of enlightenment and are used as an aid to devotion and understanding.

The action of producing a mandala is in itself an act of mindfulness and concentration. Sometimes mandalas are produced for a festival or other special occasion and may be destroyed afterwards. The very act of destroying something that has taken many hours to put together is meant to illustrate two things: first the fact that everything is impermanent; and secondly, the idea that the action of creating the mandala should be of value in itself and not merely as a means to an end. If it were not so, then one could be tempted to cling to the mandala and it would therefore become a cause of suffering. Instead, by creating and letting go, the mandala provides a symbolic representation of the whole Buddhist path.

One of the most popular mandalas is that of the Five Buddhas. Introduced in the eighth century CE, the five Buddhas (Vairocana, who displays the teaching mudra; Aksobya, representing unshakeable determination; Ratnasambhava, generously offering riches; Amitabha, representing compassion; and Amoghasiddhi, representing effective action) each represent an aspect of the universe and the human response to it. Each has a distinctive colour and mudra (hand position), is associated with a particular animal, and represents a quality of enlightenment. These transcendent Buddhas are quite unlike earlier images, which served as a focus for devotion to the historical Buddha. Here, the mandala is a symbolic representation of the whole of reality, showing how Buddhist wisdom encounters every aspect of life.

see also...

Tibetan Buddhism; Worship

Mantras

The rational mind has its limitations and Buddhism has several techniques for getting beyond them. One of these is the use of mantras. A mantra is a phrase, generally in Sanskrit, that is chanted repeatedly. The syllables which make up the mantra do not need to make sense grammatically, for a mantra does not work on a rational level. Rather, it is intended to invoke a particular Buddha figure or quality. Sometimes Buddhists chant a mantra at the same time as visualizing the corresponding Buddha image.

Thus, mantras are used rather as an aid to, or an alternative to, meditation. They evoke a quality of the enlightened mind and help the person using them to enter into that quality in a gentle and imaginative way. There is no point in trying to ask for a rational explanation of them, nor is much gained by a translation of each of the syllables – although sometimes they do indeed give an overall impression of the Buddha quality evoked.

Best known of all mantras is 'Om-mani-padme-hum' the mantra of Avalokiteshvara, Bodhisattva of Compassion. It is used very widely among Tibetan Buddhists. Of the syllables mani means 'jewel', and padme is 'lotus'. Avalokiteshvara is sometimes referred to as 'the jewel in the lotus'. Whether written up, displayed on prayer flags or chanted over and over during everyday activities, this mantra is a key feature of Tibetan Buddhism.

All the popular Buddha and Bodhisattva figures have their own mantras and the pace and tones in which they are chanted express their particular characters. Some branches of Buddhism use chanting rather than meditation as their normal form of spiritual practice. Nichiren Buddhists, and other groups following that tradition, chant the mantra 'Nam-myoho-renge-kyo', which acknowledges the 'Perfect Law of the Lotus Sutra'. Some greet one another with the mantra, which to the unwary can cause some confusion!

see also...

Nichiren; Pure Land Buddhism; Tibetan Buddhism

Mara and Yama

Buddhism is never short of fearful images, nor does it hold back from facing up to that which threatens human life. It often seems to delight in them, in order to shock people into taking a radical look at the human situation. One such image is of Mara, who is seen as the personification of destruction and whose name means 'death' and also Yama, the bringer of death. Mara is not a personal devil, in the Western sense, but serves to represent all that prevents people from following the spiritual path, or that keeps them locked into the cycle of craving and rebirth.

There are two occasions where Mara or Yama features prominently:

1. Mara is portrayed as trying to distract Siddhartha from his quest for enlightenment as he sat beneath the Bo Tree, first by presenting him with fearful images and then tempting him by sexual ones (the 'Daughters of Mara'). Mara therefore expresses the two key forces – fear on the one hand and lust on the other – that hinder progress. It is in overcoming both of these in his determination to achieve enlightenment, that the Buddha is said to have vanquished Mara.
2. Yama appears around the outside of the traditional Wheel of Life image, as the devil figure who holds the whole world in his claws. The Wheel of Life maps out the way in which, through greed, hatred and ignorance, life is trapped into a succession of births, and around its outer rim are the *nidanas*, the links which show the outworking of kamma. In other words, the Wheel of Life depicts the state in which the unenlightened inevitably find themselves. It is the longings and fears represented by Yama that keep that whole process going, keeping creatures bound by craving to the sufferings of the rounds of existence.

see also...

Death; Shakyamuni Buddha; Twelve Links; Wheel of Life

Marks of Existence

The Buddha described three universal features, or marks (*Lakshana* in Sanskrit), of existence: *anicca*, *anatta* and *dukkha*:

Anicca (all compound things are subject to change) – this is the basic idea of *paticcasamupada* ('interconnectedness', or 'dependent origination'), and is confirmed by observation. Everything exists within a flow of changes and causes. Existence is not a matter of permanent things, each with its own fixed essence, being related to one another in some mechanical fashion; rather, existence is a flow which has neither beginning nor end, and in which elements come together in temporary arrangements, including ourselves and everything we know.

Anatta (there is no essential or permanent self) follows from anicca. If everything is put together, with its various elements related and caused by things other than itself, then it cannot claim to be in any way self-contained or permanent. Both human beings and everything else lack a permanent essence.

Dukkha (unsatisfactoriness) – because everything will change, decay and pass out of existence, and the attempt to pretend that this is not the case (for example, by clinging to things and wanting them to be unchanging) is the cause of further suffering.

The marks of existence, although experienced negatively by the unwise, have positive implications. Anicca and anatta imply that development and change is possible. Without them, people would be unable to change their circumstances. Buddhism recognizes the cumulative effect of positive action in producing causes and conditions which influence the future for good. Even dukkha can serve a positive purpose. By focusing on the mental conditions that lead to suffering, and by offering a way to counter them, Buddhism offers a way to engage positively in this changing and interconnected world.

see also...

Anatta; Dukkha; Impermanence; Interconnectedness

Meditation

Buddhism aims to overcome suffering and offers a way both of looking at life (wisdom) and behaving (ethics) that are intended to overcome unskilful ways of thinking and behaving. However, this is not enough if a person's thoughts and feelings are not also controlled and directed in a positive way. The means of producing and maintaining positive mental states is meditation (which thus becomes the third part of the Buddhist 'triple way').

There are two forms of meditation (dhyana): samatha and vipassana, the former leading to calmness and integration, the latter encouraging a deeper 'insight' into reality. Meditation is performed generally sitting on a cushion or stool, with careful attention to posture to ensure comfort and balance. There is also walking meditation, often used in conjunction with sitting meditation during long sessions.

Zen is the Japanese equivalent of the Sanskrit 'dhyana', and therefore Zen Buddhism is literally 'meditation Buddhism', with Za-Zen as central to its practice. An important feature of meditation is mindfulness, a quality which is encouraged as a permanent state, rather than one experienced in meditation sessions only. Mindfulness of Breathing is an early form of meditation, outlined in the sutras. A popular form of meditation, described by Buddhaghosa, consists of entering imaginatively into the Four Sublime States, the Brahma Viharas, evoking loving-kindness, compassion, joy and equanimity.

Meditation may consist of clearing the mind of concepts and images, or may involve visualization. As meditation deepens, one may pass through one or more of the traditional stages of meditative absorption, known as the dhyanas. Although positive in terms of a sense of fulfilment and integration, these are not seen as ends in themselves. In fact, all meditation is merely a means of cultivating positive mental states, which are then able to influence the rest of one's life.

see also...

Mindfulness; Samatha Meditation; Vipassana Meditation; Za-zen

Metta (Loving-Kindness)

It would be impossible to develop genuine compassion or generosity without having a sense of love for all creatures. The Buddhist term for love is *metta* – the first of the four Brahma Viharas (along with compassion, joy and equanimity) which Buddhists seek to cultivate.

Since clinging or craving is the root cause of suffering, it is important that metta is not confused with the emotional love that simply reflects a need of the loved object. Metta has to be a non-clinging form of love, in order that other Buddhist qualities may spring from it. Without this, compassion, for example, would not be separated from self-interest and can descend into 'do-gooding'.

A popular form of meditation is the *metta bhavana*, or meditation on loving-kindness. In practice it takes the form of imaginatively moving outwards, from oneself, a good friend, a person whom is 'neutral' (for example a person one sees, but does not know and therefore has no feelings for) and then a person who is an enemy or one who irritates. From there one moves out to include all four at once, and then further out until the meditation includes all people and all living things.

At each stage one enters imaginatively in wishing that person well. It is also important to wish yourself well, since self-hatred is a barrier to understanding and loving others. Both compassion and sympathetic joy spring naturally from an attitude of loving-kindness: the former when it encounters suffering, the latter when it encounters happiness. It is the deliberate cultivation of positive states of mind, with the aim of encouraging those states to arise naturally during the rest of one's life.

see also...

Brahma Viharas; Meditation

Middle Way

There are different senses in which Buddhism may be described as the 'middle way'. The most obvious is illustrated by the life of Siddhartha Gautama prior to his enlightenment. He had experienced a life of luxury and found that it did not give him complete satisfaction. He then attempted to find the truth through self-mortification and found that it could not be achieved. Following his enlightenment, he therefore taught a way of life that was mid-way between those two extremes.

At another level, however, Buddhist teaching offers a middle way between the extremes of eternalism and nihilism. Eternalism is the view that things, ideas, and particularly 'the self' are in fact eternal, having their own inherent value and being unchangeable. Nihilism is the negative response to the fact that things begin and cease, are born and die; it sees nothing as being of any value. The Buddhist teaching of conditioned co-production (interconnectedness) is that things do indeed come into being only as a result of causes and conditions, and do not have a permanent or inherent selfhood, but that the recognition of this does not mean that they have no reality or value.

This is expressed in practical terms by attempting to be mindful of everything that is happening, monitoring and acknowledging the flow of ideas and feelings that pass through the mind, and not clinging to anything, or any idea, in the hope of absolute satisfaction or truth. The middle way does not represent compromise. It is not that people are unable to achieve some absolute goal and must therefore settle for a half-way house, but that the very idea of absolutes is a mistake. The Buddhist vision is one where everything has its place, but only within the ongoing stream of life. Everything is as it is because of everything else. In scientific terms, that may be absolutely obvious, but it is not the way most people think and feel about their lives – to do so is to approach enlightenment.

see also...

Buddha; Interconnectedness; Shakyamuni Buddha

Mindfulness

Mindfulness is the seventh step of the Noble Eightfold Path and is a central feature of Buddhism mental training. Basically, mindfulness is the ability to be aware. Ancient spiritual practices, taken over by the Buddha and his followers, include the awareness of the process of breathing – gently following each in-breath and out-breath. Such practice has two effects: it induces a sense of calm centredness, letting the mind become still and focused; it also trains the mind to give attention to the chosen object, rather than ranging from one thing to another (a traditional image of which is the monkey grasping at fruits as it swings through the jungle).

The Four Foundations of Mindfulness refer to the four areas which people may train to increase their awareness: of the body; of feelings (whether one's experience at this moment is pleasant, painful or neutral); of mental states (one's mood, or one's response to experiences); and of the objects of thought (ideas and concepts). Mindfulness relates to the central idea of interconnectedness. If everything arises as a result of conditions, it is important to be aware of exactly what is happening and one's response to it in terms of feelings and thoughts. Mindfulness is an awareness of the causes and conditions that are determining this present moment, and of how one is relating to them. Without awareness of this sort, it is difficult to see how anyone could make progress in understanding habitual patterns of thought or emotion.

Overall, mindfulness is a process of being constantly aware of the arising and passing away of states – experiences, thoughts and feelings – and recognizing that all things change and flow on in the stream of life.

Mindfulness enables a person to be aware of the arising of, say, happiness, being fully aware of it, but not responding to it by wanting to grasp or hold on to the source of that happiness. It is the gap between experience and response, that allows rational human beings to influence their own kamma (karma) and future.

see also...

Meditation

Monasticism

Like the Buddha himself, some of his followers renounced family life in order to follow the spiritual quest. The term 'Sangha' often refers to these monks and nuns, although it is used more widely of the fourfold assembly of monks, nuns, male and female lay followers. The monastic orders have been influential in the spread of Buddhism and in the transmission of its scriptures. Particularly in Theravada Buddhism, monastic life is regarded as the ideal preparation for enlightenment. There is always a period of probation before ordination, and vows are taken for a set period of time, not for life. A person can choose to leave the Order and return to family life, rejoining it at a later stage.

The monastic life seeks to follow a middle way, in that it renounces luxurious living, without seeking unnecessary hardship. Food is generally taken in a single meal, eaten before midday. Monks and nuns are wholly supported by lay Buddhists, so that they may be free to meditate, study and teach the Dhamma. In return, lay followers look to the monastic community for support and encouragement. Those who become monks or nuns accept rules over and above the basic five precepts that all Buddhists accept as training principles. Instead of simply abstaining from misuse of sexuality and the senses, he (or she) accepts the discipline of abstaining from all sexual activity. In addition they accept: not eating after midday; not attending public entertainment; not using perfumes or personal ornaments; not using a luxurious bed; not handling money. They are by tradition allowed eight things: three robes, a bowl, a razor, a needle and cotton, a drinking cup and a girdle.

Those who are preparing for the monastic life, but not yet ordained, are generally termed Samaneras. A person leaving home in order to test out their vocation for the monastic life generally takes the vows of an Anagarika (one who has entered the homeless life) for one year, as a training period.

see also...

Nuns; Sangha; Shakyamuni Buddha; Theravada; Vinaya

Morality (Sila)

Central to Buddhism is the idea that everything is interconnected, and this applies to the three principal ways of following the Buddhist path (*sila*, *samadhi* and *prajna* – morality, meditation and wisdom) as much as anything else. Meditation and wisdom are unlikely to be developed unless a person has a fundamental sense of morality. Equally, morality is not sustained unless it builds on a steady mind and sound understanding of reality. All Buddhist teaching is therefore relevant in some way to ethical and spiritual practice. Buddhism does not work on the basis of fixed rules, imposed from outside with rewards or punishments. Rather, it suggests that progress will be made only by following basic moral precepts, of which lay people accept five – to avoid killing, stealing, misuse of the sense, false speech and intoxication.

Owing to the fact that circumstances are always changing, Buddhists do not tend to say that actions are right or wrong (since, what is right for one person might be wrong for another), but skilful or unskilful – depending on whether or not it promotes love, generosity and wisdom. Whether an action is skilful or not does not depend on the results it achieves, but on the intention of the person who performs it. Buddhist morality is personal – a conscious response to a situation; it is not based simply on an assessment of predicted results. Morality is also closely linked to the idea of kamma (karma). In the ordinary course of events, if a person sees something desirable, the immediate reaction is to want it. If this leads to an unhealthy craving, the result may be harmful. The aim of Buddhist practice is to get beyond that pattern of unthinking stimulus and response, injecting an element of freedom and choice. Of course, that does not mean that one rejects what is enjoyable (Buddhists can enjoy themselves as much as anyone else), but one's enjoyment is freely chosen, and has consequences – good or bad – which colour one's future experience.

see also...

Kamma; Precepts; Skilful Means; Twelve Links

Mudras

Buddhist images are full of symbolism, reflecting different aspects of the enlightenment experience, or qualities that Buddhists seek to develop. The hand gestures of Buddha images are termed *mudras*, and each has a particular meaning. They include the earth-touching mudra (the *Bhumisparsha*), in which the Buddha is shown sitting in meditation with his right hand touching the ground in front of him. This refers to the account of his enlightenment when he was said to call upon the Earth goddess to witness his preparation for Buddhahood over many lifetimes. It conveys a sense of solidarity and rootedness. Sometimes the Buddha is shown with hands together on his lap in the position used for meditation, sometimes his right hand is raised in an expression of fearlessness and strength. Hands held in front of the body, as though turning a small invisible wheel, is the teaching mudra, recalling the expression used for the Buddha's first sermon – 'the first turning of the wheel of the Dharma'.

Not only are mudras shown as images, but they are also acted out, especially in Tantric Buddhism. If everything is interconnected, then the postures people adopt physically can evoke and stimulate the corresponding emotions. This is, of course, a universal phenomenon, from warlike dances of primitive tribes or New Zealand rugby players, to the patterns of animal courtship. In Buddhism, however, it applies to the sequence of mudras in a Tantric rite, and also to the adoption of an upright and balanced position for meditation.

As with all Buddhist practice, it is important to remember that actions and postures are not seen as of value in themselves, they are all aimed at evoking positive mental states. Thus, the mudras of a Tantric performance are not – as might be seen to be the case in ceremonies and offering made in Hindu worship – either sacred or effective in themselves; the key to their value is in the attitude and mindfulness of the person who performs them.

see also...

Images; Tantra; Tibetan Buddhism

Nibbana (Nirvana)

Nibbana may be described as the goal of the Buddhist life. It is a state in which the triple fires of greed, hatred and ignorance have no more fuel and are therefore extinguished. They are replaced by a state of bliss, comprising generosity, love and insight. It is therefore a point at which suffering is at an end. Nibbana is an ethical state that a Buddhist aspires to achieve in this life. It is *not* the same as extinction. Since one derivation of nibbana is 'to blow out' it has sometimes mistakenly been thought of as extinction, but it is the fuel which supplies the triple fire that is exhausted and the fire therefore extinguished.

The important thing about nibbana is that it is outside the chain of conditioned co-production – in other words, it is outside the realm of karma. It is not caused directly by anything else, and is therefore a state quite outside the normal experiences of life. Another translation of nibbana is 'liberation', meaning that the person has achieved liberation from the binding forces of the fetters that hold other people in check. One who has achieved nibbana is termed an Arhat.

Notice that a person who has achieved nibbana continues to live in this ordinary world and will eventually die like everyone else. It is not an escape, but a new quality of response to the world, freed from the triple fires. In the case of the Buddha, he is described as passing at his death into a state of *parinirvana*, or 'complete' nibbana. Being fully enlightened, and generating no more karma, it is thought that he thus passes completely beyond the realm of rebecoming or rebirth. However, he refused to speculate on whether such a person should be said to either exist or not exist after death.

Nibbana is also described as the 'fearless state' – that one is able to face everything and understand everything, without the fear that comes from the narrow (and ultimately fruitless) quest for self-protection.

see also...

Arhats; Buddha Nature; Craving; Enlightenment

Nichiren Buddhism

This form of Buddhism was founded by Nichiren Daishonin (1222–82), a Japanese monk. He was a very colourful and outspoken character, intensely patriotic and critical of the government of his day, which led him to be imprisoned, almost executed, and exiled. Nichiren Buddhism, following the Pure Land tradition, has chanting rather than meditation as its main spritual practice. Nichiren took the Lotus Sutra as the basis of his teaching, and therefore encouraged his followers to chant 'Nam-myoho-renge-kyo'. 'Nam' is a word meaning devotion or dedications, and 'myoho-renge-kyo' is 'the mystic law of the Lotus Sutra'. Many Nichiren Buddhists also greet one another with this phrase and, because they tend to say it very quickly, it can confuse non-Buddhists!

Nichren Buddhism is practical and looks for results in terms of added success and happiness in life. It encourages people to try chanting and to test out its teachings, to see if it makes any different to their lives. When Nichiren Buddhists chant, they do so in front of a small scroll called a Gohonzon, on which is inscribed Chinese and Sanskrit characters, representing enlightenment. The Gohonzon is used as a focus of attention for devotion and chanting. Nichiren Buddhists take the view that, in chanting, they are sending out vibrations which will have a beneficial effect throughout the world. Because of the importance for them of the Lotus Sutra, many learn portions of it by heart and recite them before their Gohonzon.

The second half of the twentieth century, saw the rapid growth of an international lay society known as Sokka Gakkai, meaning 'value creating society'. Its name reflects the general attitude of Nichiren Buddhism that one should seek to overcome practical problems and to strive to create the greatest value possible from every situation. It has therefore had a powerful appeal to those who naturally seek to be creative and maximize every possibility in life, both personally and globally.

see also...

Japanese Buddhism; Lotus Sutra

Non-violence (Ahimsa)

Not taking life is the first of the Buddhist precepts, and is absolutely fundamental both to Buddhist ethics and to its overall view of the world. It is a moral ideal shared also by Hindus and particularly by Jains. In Buddhist teaching, it follows from the fundamental awareness that all things are interconnected.

The Buddha simply pointed out that all creatures fear death and seek to avoid suffering and pain. One who seeks that for himself or herself, should therefore do everything possible to see that no such suffering is imposed on others. There is also the more general sense that the Buddhist should live in a way that is harmless.

The positive side of the first precept is the cultivation of loving-kindness (*metta*) and compassion towards all living things. This requires the principle of *ahimsa* towards animals as well as humans. Consequently, there is a long tradition of vegetarianism within Buddhism. On the other hand, food should not be wasted and if a monk or nun is offered food that includes meat or fish, the general principle is that it should be eaten. There is an absolute prohibition on a monk or nun knowingly allowing any creature to be killed especially in order to provide food for oneself.

In the East, the majority of Buddhists are not strict vegetarians. In any case, there are parts of the world where lack of good land for the cultivation of crops makes a vegetarian diet very difficult.

The Buddha, in establishing The Middle Way, was opposed to spiritual practices that deliberately set out to cause suffering to one's own body. Therefore a Buddhist should apply the principle of Ahimsa to himself or herself, as well as to other creatures.

see also...

Morality; Precepts

Nuns

The Buddha made it clear that he believed that women and men were equally capable of reaching liberation, and the scriptures record many women having done so. However, when it came to establishing an order of nuns (bhikkhunis), the Buddha had major reservations for practical and social reasons. Apart from anything else, in the society of his day women were very much under the authority of men, first their father, then their husband and finally, if widowed, their son or sons.

However, after a determined effort on the part of Maha Pajapati Gotami (his aunt and foster mother), joined later by Rahula-Mata (his former wife) and many other Sakyan women, the Buddha agreed that an order of nuns should be established. They were to agree to eight special rules, which effectively put them under the authority of the male Sangha, but which were clearly also aimed at preventing scandal, offering some measure of protection, and preventing women from entering the order simply to gain social prestige. In practice, nuns met with some opposition and there are accounts of them being thrown out of houses, called 'shaven-headed whores', and one case of a nun living in Angharana Forest being raped. Nevertheless, it is difficult today to appreciate what a radical step it was for women to assert themselves and to embark on the religious ascetic life – a step that had been seen previously as belonging exclusively to men, and given a high status.

Nuns who had been ordained for ten years, took the title Theri (Elder), like their male colleagues, and the scriptures give accounts of nuns with particular skills in scholarship. However, the order of nuns had difficulties surviving, especially in time of war, and in the tenth century the order finally died out. It was not re-started, since a nun cannot be ordained by a monk, but only by another nun. Within Theravada countries, therefore, there are no fully ordained nuns in the original sense. However, the modern equivalent of the bhikkhuni is the *upasika*. Wearing white robes and with shaved heads, upasikas follow the same lifestyle as bhikkhus, but have less status.

see also...

Monasticism

Pali

By the time the Buddha died, there was a well-established oral tradition, both of the Vinaya (the rules for monastic life) and of the Sutta (the teachings). This oral tradition continued for 400 years. It appears that the Buddha and his early followers resisted the temptation to present the Dhamma in Sanskrit, the language used for Hindu scriptures, believing that it was important for the teachings to remain in the languages of the common people, rather than formalized.

In the first century BCE, however, the scriptures were written down in Sri Lanka, using a language and script called Pali, closely related to the original language of the Buddha. This is known as the Pali Canon and forms the scriptures of the Theravada tradition. The Mahayana and Vajrayana also accept these, but have their own scriptures as well, generally in Sanskrit, Tibetan or Chinese.

The Pali Canon is also known as Tipitaka (Pali) or Tripitaka (Sanskrit), meaning 'three baskets', since it is divided into three sections:

1 **The Vinaya Pitaka** contains the rules for monks, along with appropriate disciplinary measures that should be taken if they are broken, and various details concerning the ordering of monastic life, including how to admit people to the order, how to organize retreats and so on.
2 **The Sutta Pitaka** is the collection of the teachings of the Buddha, arranged in five sections, largely according to the length of the dialogues. Shorter sayings are grouped according to topics, or arranged numerically. The Sutta Pitaka includes such works as the Jataka Tales about former lives of the Buddha, and the ever-popular Dhammapada.
3 **The Abhidhamma Pitaka** contains a more philosophical analysis of the Buddha's teachings, arranged in seven sections, composed in the third century BCE in an attempt to systematize the teachings and establish an authoritative interpretation.

see also...

Abhidhamma; Dhammapada; Jataka Tales; Scriptures; Sutras; Theravada

Paramitars

Buddhism seems full of lists: three poisons, four noble truths, five precepts, five skandhas, eightfold path, twelve links and so on. They are valuable for memorizing the teachings, but they should not be taken in an exclusive way. The six *paramitars* (or 'perfections') are simply one of the ways of looking at the Buddhist path. They represent the qualities of an enlightened mind and, particularly within Mahayana Buddhism, the cultivation of these qualities is a sign of following the path of the Bodhisattva.

The six paramitars are:

1. *Dana* (generosity). This is a quality that is fundamental to all Buddhist traditions. In some it is shown particularly in making offerings to monks and nuns. Its cultivation is the positive aspect of the second precept – not stealing or taking what is not freely given.
2. *Sila* (morality). Embodied particularly in the precepts, this refers to the general awareness of self and others, and the ability to respond in a positive and freely chosen way. It is basic to all Buddhist practice and related to the idea of karma.
3. *Virya* (energy). This is seen particularly as energy that is directed towards what is good; promoting positive action alongside insight and meditation.
4. *Kshanti* (patience). Buddhism promotes equanimity (the fourth of the Brahma Viharas), not in the sense of indifference to life, but as a balanced appreciation of both the positive and negative aspects of experience. Patience flows from this, as an understanding of the limitations of others, and of the conditioned and limited nature of all things.
5. *Samadhi* (meditation). This, of course, is a feature of all Buddhist traditions; without calming and focusing the mind, it is difficult to make progress either in understanding or acting skilfully.
6. *Prajna* (wisdom). Again, this is a basic feature of all Buddhist teaching. It does not refer to academic knowledge, but to a personal understanding and appreciation of those features of reality to which the Buddha pointed.

see also...

Bodhisattva; Mahayana Buddhism; Morality; Wisdom

Philosophies

Some religions are particularly dogmatic, and those who challenge the literal truth of particular doctrines may be excluded or executed. Buddhism does not take that approach, but is generally tolerant of differences of expression of the Dhamma, or spiritual practices. Thus, for example, during the second half of the first millennium CE, there would have been monks and teachers in the same monasteries or universities following both Hinayana and Mahayana traditions, and some including tantra in their practice. Divisions in the early Sangha were generally about matters of monastic discipline, not about philosophy. However, this flexibility led to a great variety of different philosophies and traditions – for example between the early 'Hinayana' schools (of which the Theravada is the sole remaining example) and the Mahayana.

Even within the Mahayana there are major differences of philosophy, notably between the Madhyamaka and the Yogacara. The Madhyamaka, founded in the second century CE by the famous Nagarjuna, expounds the ideas of the 'Perfection of Wisdom' sutras, and places great emphasis on *shunyata* (emptiness). He made the important distinction between absolute truth (that everything is empty of inherent existence) and the conventional or relative truths about the things we encounter, which are real, but radically impermanent. Beneath its surface, the more profound truth is of emptiness. A very different approach is taken by the Yogacara, founded in the fourth century CE by Asanga and Vasubandhu. This (like the idealist philosophies in Western thought) takes as its basis the idea that everything we experience is in fact the product of our mind. This was based particularly on meditation traditions and saw itself as offering a more positive view of reality than the Madhyamaka.

For all its variety, Buddhism does not regard philosophy as an end in itself. It is always required to relate to and underpin the practical issues of meditation and morality.

see also...

Abhidhamma; Mahayana; Shunyata

Poisons

Buddhism is always keen to point out those things that prevent people from being happy, so that they can develop a critical awareness of them. Various poisonous attitudes are listed – two groups of three and one group of five:

In the middle of the Wheel of Life there are three creatures: a cock (representing greed), a snake (representing hatred) and a pig (representing ignorance). These are sometimes referred to as the three mental poisons, and they are seen to feed on one another. Together they provide the impetus to keep the wheel of conditioned existence turning and maintain its suffering.

There are also three types of craving that may be seen as poisons or taints (*astravas* in Sanskrit): craving for sense experience, in the sense of grasping at things experienced as pleasurable (*kamastrava* – *kama* being easily remembered because of the Hindu book on pleasure, the *Kama Sutra*!); craving for forms of existence, in the sense of wanting to 'be something' (*bhavastrava*); and craving to be extinct, or to remain in spiritual ignorance (*avidyastrava*).

There is also a set of five mental poisons: distractedness, anger, craving, conceit and ignorance. Since Buddhist teaching seeks to give practical help, there is a corresponding form of meditation suitable for countering each of these poisons. For a wayward mind that spins off distractedly, it prescribes the Mindfulness of Breathing, a Samatha practice, focusing gently on the breath and inducing calm and one-pointedness of mind. For anger, it prescribes the cultivation of *metta*, or loving-kindness. For craving, one can meditate on death, or visit and sit in a cremation ground – a reminder of the futility of grasping at things in order to feel secure. For conceit, one meditates that all the elements that make up oneself are actually taken from, belong to and are shared with the external world. For ignorance, one is encouraged to look at the nidanas, the links in the chain of kamma (karma).

see also...

Kamma; Wheel of Life

Prayer Wheels and Flags

A distinctive feature of Tibetan Buddhism is its use of prayer wheels and flags. There are small prayer wheels which people hold in their hands, turning them like football rattles. Larger ones are fixed into racks along walls, and sometimes one can walk past rows of these turning each of them. There are even some that are turned by water wheels. Whatever their size and use, the theory is the same: prayers, mantras or short passages of scripture are copied out and placed within them and as the wheels are turned, the mantras go round and merit is gained.

Similarly, prayer flags have Buddhist inscriptions written on them, they flutter in the wind, constantly expressing what is written on them. By far the most popular mantra, inscribed on many prayer flags and in wheels is 'Om mani padme hum', the mantra of the Bodhisattva Avalokiteshvara.

This use of flags and wheels may seem odd, until it is recognized that, for Buddhism, intentions are all-important. A person setting a mantra blowing in the wind, intends that the reality of compassion expressed in it shall spread throughout the world. A person can chant a mantra for only a limited amount of time. A constantly turning wheel is a reminder that the chant permeates everything without ceasing. Also, seeing wheels and flags is a constant reminder of the reality of what is written on them, they are therefore a skilful means of keeping the spiritual path in people's minds. In this sense, they work without resorting to magic.

see also...

Avalokiteshvara; Mantras; Tibetan Buddhism

Precepts

There are five basic moral precepts, to be used as principles of training for all Buddhists, both those in monastic order and those who are householders. They are:

1 To abstain from taking life.
2 To abstain from taking what is not freely given.
3 To abstain from misuse of the senses.
4 To abstain from speaking falsely.
5 To abstain from intoxicants that cloud the mind.

For each of these negative commitments, there are positive equivalents: to cultivate loving-kindness, generosity, simplicity and contentment in living, truthfulness and clarity of mind.

There are two other sets of precepts (one with eight and one with ten) which are accepted by some Buddhists on a permanent basis and others on special occasions – for example, during festival days. In addition to these precepts, of course, there are the numerous rules of the Vinaya that are accepted by those who become monks or nuns.

Note that precepts are not rules, handed down by some external deity, or enforced by the threat of punishment. They are simply guidelines by which individuals may assess and adapt their behaviour in line with Buddhist insights. Actions are judged according to the intention involved and the circumstances. Buddhists are expected to use skilful means to judge what is the best thing to do in any situation. Although rewards and punishments are not the motivation for keeping to the precepts, the principle of *kamma* (or *karma* in Sanskrit) implies that action in line with the precepts will bring about positive results.

In popular Buddhist culture, this leads to the idea of *punna* (merit) which may be accumulated as a result of skilful actions. To prevent the idea of gathering merit leading to selfishness, it is common (for example, at the end of a *puja*, or act of devotion) to dedicate the merit gained by performing that action to the welfare of all beings, rather than retaining it for oneself.

see also...

Morality; Skilful Means

Pure Land Buddhism

Pure Land Buddhism is based on devotion to Amida Buddha, who is seen as eternal life and infinite light. It is believed that Amida Buddha is able to create a pure land, in which all obstacles to spiritual development are removed, when people chant his name with absolute sincerity.

For Pure Land Buddhism, Amida Buddha, and indeed the very act of chanting, becomes identified with reality itself, and an expression of universal compassion. Notice how very different this is from those forms of Buddhism which focus on rational analysis and mindfulness as a path to enlightenment. Here absolute devotion is the key feature of spiritual practice.

Developed in China in the fourth century (to which it had been brought from Northern India, probably from about the second century CE), this 'Pure Land' form of Buddhism was known as *Chin t'u*. In Japan, devotion to Amida led to the founding of two major traditions, the Pure Land School founded by Honen in 1175 (Jodo), and that of Shinran Shonin (1173–1262), Jodo Shin-shu. The former recite 'Namu Amida Butsu' (Greeting, Amida Buddha) many times each day; it becomes a natural response in everything they do. The latter group tend to shorten this phrase to 'Nembutsu'.

Because the grace of Amida is all that is required, Pure Land Buddhism sees no benefit in adopting an ascetic or monastic lifestyle. Jodo Shin religious leaders can marry and do secular work alongside their religious duties, helping them to identify with ordinary people and to share the responsibilities that they have for work and family. One difficulty with this approach is that, by accommodating to the norms of society, any distinctiveness of Buddhism seems to vanish. This may seem a problem from a distinctively religious point of view, but within Buddhist practice, the recognition of the specialness and adequacy of ordinary life is found in many traditions.

see also...

Amitabha; Chinese Buddhism; Japanese Buddhism

Re-becoming

The Buddha taught that all things are interconnected, arise in dependence on conditions, and lack permanent or inherent existence (*anatta*). Therefore, unlike the Hindu idea of reincarnation, there is no fixed 'self' (or *atman*) to go from one life to another. Rather, there is a constant process of change through life. A person's thoughts of today shape what he or she will become tomorrow. This is known as *punabhava* (re-becoming). Its mechanism is *kamma* (*karma*), by which actions have consequences (good or bad). This process continues throughout life and therefore, at death, there will be kamma for which the consequences have not yet come to fruition. Buddhists believe that such kamma will influence future lives.

This does not imply that the individual reappears in a future life to experience their kamma, for that would imply the existence of a permanent self. It is just that there will be a future life that takes on the consequences of present action. The process is generally described by the image of one flame lighting another. The two flames are not one and the same (the first does not simply become the second), but the second comes into being because of the first, whilst remaining distinct from it.

At his enlightenment, the Buddha is said to have become aware of all his former lives. Some of these are depicted in the Jataka Tales, in which the Buddha-to-be performs acts of kindness and self-sacrifice, in both human and animal lives, gradually preparing himself for enlightenment. These are seen as phases in the life that was to become the Buddha. Speculation is generally discouraged and the Buddha refused to say whether a Tathagata (one who has become enlightened) existed or did not exist after death, but in Tibetan Buddhism, it is believed that senior lamas can influence their future birth, and a search is made for the karmic successor, called a *tulku*.

see also...

Anatta; Jataka Tales; Kamma; Tulku

Refuges

The very starting point of the Buddha's teaching is that people suffer because they are constantly engaged in the hopeless quest for things to give them absolute and permanent happiness and make them feel secure. In a world where everything is interconnected and constantly changing, finding a guaranteed refuge from the awareness of one's own mortality and limitations simply isn't possible.

Faced with the uncertainties of life, one may be tempted to 'go to refuge' to one's career, or money, or to one's lover or friend, or to an abstract idea like democracy, in order to find security. However, ultimately, none of these is going to be permanent or sufficient. The starting point of the religious quest is therefore the recognition of the inadequacy of mundane refuges.

At the beginning of many acts of worship, at festivals and on other special occasions, Buddhists may recite the 'refuges and precepts' before an ordained member of the monastic community. Indeed, taking the refuges and precepts is the accepted way of becoming a Buddhist. The precepts refer to the five moral precepts common to all Buddhists, the refuges to which a Buddhist goes are the Buddha, the Dhamma (his teaching) and the Sangha (the community of his followers). These refuges are contrasted with the mundane variety.

To go for refuge to the Buddha is not simply to trust an historical person, but to recognize the possibility of one's own enlightenment. The Dhamma represents the teachings (not taken on trust, but there to be explored) through which one hopes to move towards enlightenment. The Sangha is the community of those with whom one shares that spiritual journey.

see also...

Buddha; Dhamma; Sangha; Worship

Samatha Meditation

In the ordinary course of events, the mind has a tendency to be constantly distracted, first to one thing then on to the next, always rushing ahead of the present moment, anticipating, evaluating and gathering new sensations. It is a situation where, bombarded with a variety of ideas from within, and experiences from without, a person is liable to suffer from permanent mental indigestion. In such circumstances, stimulus and response come so fast that it is difficult to find a gap between them for reflection and choice. Distractedness is therefore seen as one of the poisons, hindering a person from following the Buddhist path. The antidote to this is Samatha meditation. Unlike Vipassana meditation, in which a person seeks insight into particular features of life, Samatha aims at creating a mind that is stilled, calm and one-pointed.

A principal technique for achieving this is the Mindfulness of Breathing, in which a person progressively concentrates on the sensation of breath entering and leaving the body. Initially, the mind's response to this is to throw up a good number of distractions, but the meditator just acknowledges each of these and sets them aside. Nothing should be forced, for the active determination to get rid of a thought, and any anger that it has recurred, is just one more distraction. Gradually, the mind becomes progressively more able to remain calm and to enter deeply into the present experience. At this point, the meditator may enter into one of the deeper states of awareness, called the *dhyanas*. The aim of Samatha meditation is not simply to enable a person to feel good while meditating (although that, in itself, is a bonus), but to have a progressively calming effect on the rest of his or her life, making it possible to appreciate and explore other elements of Buddhist teaching.

see also...

Dhyana States; Meditation; Mindfulness; Poisons; Vipassana Meditation

Samsara

Samsara is the term used to describe the ordinary world, dominated by the endless cycle of birth and death. It is illustrated by the Wheel of Life – with the three poisons (greed, hatred and ignorance), the six realms, and the nidana links illustrating the process by which ignorance leads to further birth and death.

Samsara is the realm of change – nothing within it is permanent. It is the key feature of Samsara, that it is unsatisfactory, and that craving for anything within it only leads to suffering in the broad sense. However, Samsara is also a concept linked to spiritual practice. It is the state of craving and rebirth which can be overcome (see The Four Noble Truths), leading ultimately to Nibbana, the state of peace characterized by love, generosity and insight.

If Nibbana is a state into which a person can enter in this life, does he or she not also continue in the world of Samsara? This question led some Mahayana Buddhists to argue that Nibbana and Samsara were not two separate locations – not two different worlds – but one and the same world experienced in two different ways. To the ignorant and grasping, the world of Samsara is a source of suffering; to one who experiences Nibbana, he or she lives on, but does not experience or generate further kamma, and is not therefore subject to the negative aspect of Samsara.

Buddhism deals with what is experienced. Its starting point is that the way the world is experienced for most people is as Samsara – ignorance and craving, leading to the sufferings of further birth and death. Its goal is to release people from that experience of the world, allowing them to enter Nibbana, in which life is experienced quite differently. Samsara is thus not a location (not simply a world of space and time) but a mode of experience.

Freedom from the limitations of Samsara is called Moksha (release) – a term Buddhism shares with other Indian religious traditions.

see also...

Impermanence; Interconnectedness; Nibbana

Samskaras

Buddhist teaching sees the self as made up of five aggregates, or heaps (the *skandhas*), each of which is impermanent and changing. The fourth of these heaps is that of the samskaras (or samkharas), and it is the heap of 'mental formations'. There are 52 of these, and they include such things as attention, determination, ignorance, conceit, energy, desire and wisdom. In other words, they constitute our habitual ways of thinking and responding to life.

The samskaras play an absolutely central role in Buddhist psychology and the following of the Buddhist path. This is because it is these mental formations which determine our volitional activities – those things that we choose to do – and it is the volitional activities that form the basis of our good or bad karma. What we do with our lives, and the results that come from it, are all influenced by the samskaras.

In Western terms, the samskaras would probably be thought of as personality traits, since they show a person's habitual responses. The key feature of Buddhist psychology, however, is that the samskaras are not fixed. Like all the five skandhas that make up each person, they are constantly changing. The implication of this is that, through the application of morality, meditation and wisdom (in other words, by following the Buddhist path) we can change our habitual responses and thus change the kamma (karma) we produce. At the opening of the Dhammapada there is the blunt statement that our life is the creation of our mind, that as we think so we live – that an evil mind leads to suffering and a pure mind to happiness. This is another way of saying that the samskaras determine both what we are and what we will become.

The practice of mindfulness includes mindfulness of one's state of mind, as well as the objects of thought, and these states of mind show themselves in terms of the samskaras.

see also...

Anatta; Kamma; Skandhas

Sangha

The Sangha is the collective term for those who are followers of the Buddha. Traditionally, the Sangha was divided into four groups: bhikkhus (monks), bhikkhunis (nuns), upasakas (male lay followers) and upasikas (female lay followers). And this reflects the situation from the days of the Buddha, where some of his followers left their homes and literally followed him on his travels, gathering together in *viharas* (resting places) which eventually became settled monasteries, whilst others continued with their ordinary domestic lives.

Sometimes the term Sangha is taken to refer only to those who are ordained as monks, but it should really be used of all followers, both monastic and lay. It is clear from the scriptures that the Buddha intended his teaching to be relevant both to those who had 'gone forth' from the life of the householder, and to lay people and, among the latter, both those who were celibate and those who lived the family life. They were all seen as flowing, like a great river, towards the spiritual goal of *Nibbana* (*Nirvana*), and progress towards that was recognized in large numbers of followers of all categories.

There is also the *Arya Sangha* (or 'noble' Sangha), a term used for those who have become Arhats (in the early and Theravada traditions) and Bodhisattvas (in Mahayana Buddhism) – a kind of spiritual elite which others are inspired to follow.

The Sangha is, of course, the third of the 'refuges' to which Buddhists go when they recite the 'refuges and precepts'. In most Buddhist traditions, lay people are advised to be guided in their practice by a more senior member of the Sangha, and this is particularly the case with tantric practices, which one is not encouraged to try without guidance. In the most general sense, of course, going for refuge to the Sangha reflects the need for and value of spiritual friendship in following the Buddhist path.

see also...

Monasticism; Refuges; Tantra

Satori

Zen speaks of moments of insight called *satori*, when a person has a kind of spiritual breakthrough in the quest for enlightenment. Satori is said to happen suddenly, not as a result of slow preparation. This sounds as if no effort or preparation is needed in order to be enlightened, but that would be wrong. The idea of satori is that the moment of enlightenment takes place outside time altogether. One cannot do anything to achieve satori, one can only set up the conditions in which one hopes it might arise.

In a traditional story illustrating this, a teacher takes a brick and starts rubbing it. When the student asks what he is doing, he replies that he is trying to turn it into a mirror. The student recognizes that it is quite impossible. The teacher then makes the point that effort in sitting meditation in itself will not produce enlightenment.

In other words, enlightenment is not part of a mechanical process, it is not an effect of which something else is the direct cause. Nor is it the result of merit that can be accumulated; it is the sudden recognition of things just as they are. In this sense, satori is in line with the older Buddhist traditions about enlightenment. The Buddha did not achieve enlightenment as a result of his earlier ascetic practice, but only at the point at which he was able to let go of that practice.

One of the key features of Zen is that, to the enlightened mind, everything remains exactly as it is. There are not two worlds, one seen by those who are enlightened and another representing the world of everyday experience. The same thing that becomes a matter of wonder to the enlightened, remains ordinary to the person who has not been so enlightened.

see also...

Enlightenment; Zen

Scriptures

Buddhist scriptures can be divided between Buddhavacana – the term for records of the teachings of Buddha Shakyamuni (the *sutras*) – and later commentaries on the Buddhist path, written by his followers.

The teachings of the Buddha were memorized and transmitted, largely within the monastic community, before being set down in written form. The earliest existing set of written scriptures are the Theravada Pali Canon, dating from the first century BCE. It comprises what is known as the Tripitaka (or 'three baskets'): the Sutta Pitaka is a collection of the teachings of the Buddha, mainly in the form of dialogues between the Buddha and those who came to see him; the Vinaya Pitaka is a detailed set of rules for the monastic community; and the Abhidhamma Pitaka is a set of philosophical treatises, giving detailed analyses of experience and summary lists of concepts that appear also in the Suttas. The Mahayana scriptures, generally written in Sanskrit, are mainly of a later date, although they claim that their teachings originate in those of Shakyamuni Buddha. Of these, probably the most widely revered is The Lotus Sutra, which has a massive cosmic vision of world systems (in each of which a Buddha is teaching), as well as memorable stories to illustrate the Buddhist path.

Many of the Mahayana scriptures, although possibly originating from India and written in Sanskrit, were preserved in Chinese translation after the originals were lost. Written copies of the scriptures are treated with great respect within the Buddhist tradition, but their use varies considerably. In many traditions the individual's own experience and relationship with a spiritual teacher takes precedence over systematic study of scriptures.

In the process of study, there are three levels: that which comes from reading and hearing; that which is personally integrated and understood; and that which is known through the process of reflection and meditation.

see also...

Dhammapada; Lotus Sutra; Pali; Sutras

Shakyamuni Buddha

Although Buddhist philosophy and practice is now immensely varied, it originated in the distinctive and original teaching of one man – Siddhattha Gotama (or Siddhartha Gautama in Sanskrit). He lived in northern India, at around 563–483 BCE. Although larger kingdoms were established in the area at that time, there were also autonomous tribal units, each with a small number of ruling families. Siddhartha was born the son of a local ruler of the Shakya tribe and the title 'Shakyamuni', often used of the historical Buddha, translates as 'wise man of the Shakyas'.

He is said to have been brought up in some luxury and that his father sought to insulate him from suffering and the harsher realities of life. He married a local princess (Yasodara), who bore him a son (Rahula). Certainly, later in life, he appears to have known and been on good terms with the local kings and ruling families, receiving considerable support from them.

At the age of 29, having become aware of old age, sickness, death and the religious quest to understand and overcome them (through what are referred to as the 'four sights'), he left home and adopted the religious life of a wandering ascetic. Following six years of traditional meditation and strict ascetic practices, during which time he had failed to achieve the insight he sought, he experienced what is described as his enlightenment, following which he is referred to as Buddha (the 'enlightened one'). He then embarked on more than 40 years of travelling and teaching, gathering around him a large number of disciples, some of whom joined him in the homeless life, others continuing to live as householders. Many of the sutras describe incidents when individuals or groups approached the Buddha for advice.

He died of food poisoning at Kusinara at the age of 80, by which time the monastic Sangha was well established and his teachings had been clearly formulated and committed to memory by his principal followers.

see also...

Buddha; Four Sights; Sangha

Shrines

It is sometimes difficult to know how to categorize Buddhism. Is is a philosophy? A system of ethics? A religion? Because it does not require belief in God, and because it invites people to examine and assess its teachings for themselves, it is tempting to see it as a guide to happiness that requires thought and effort, but not commitment or devotion. How do you reconcile this with what goes on at a Buddhist shrine?

A shrine has one or more statues (*rupas*) of the Buddha and may have a range of Buddha or Bodhisattva images, either in the form of rupas, or as *thankas* hanging on the wall. In front of the Buddha figure there will probably be a row of seven small bowls containing water, representing the traditional offerings made to an honoured guest. There will also be offerings that people have made – often in the form of lighted candles, flowers, incense and food.

Worshippers bow before the image or prostrate themselves on the floor. There may be chanting or the shrine room may be used for meditation. Many Buddhists have small shrines at home. At first sight, all this follows the pattern of other religions, with devotion being paid to the Buddha as though to a god. The devotional aspects of Buddhism developed particularly during the middle centuries of the first millennium CE and are found, to a greater or lesser extent, in all branches. Clearly, the development and use of shrines reflects a deep human spiritual need, enabling the engagement of the senses and the emotions as well as the mind. For Buddhism, it is the intention that matters and if a person is helped by devotional practices, that is all well and good.

Shrines vary considerably from the plain to the highly ornate, from one that has a single Buddha image, or a stupa, to one that contains a great variety of Buddha and Bodhisattva images, particularly in the Mahayana and Vajrayana traditions.

see also...

Images; Thankas; Worship

Shunyata

All Buddhist teaching emphasizes that individual things, however we may speak about them conventionally, are actually devoid of inherent existence. They are merely 'put together' on a temporary basis. In Mahayana Buddhism, this is expressed by using the term shunyata. This is normally translated as 'emptiness', but that does not really convey its meaning. It is really a matter of being empty of a conventional or permanent sense of self. The 'emptiness' at the heart of reality is something undifferentiated, something in which everything shares, something which frees individual things from their separateness and therefore their ultimate sense of loss and being finite.

Shunyata cannot be described. If it could, it would become a conventional thing alongside others – which is exactly what it is trying to get away from. Shunyata is what appears once you stop trying to give descriptions, once you get beyond the 'this' and 'that' of experience and enter into what lies behind the apparent separateness of things.

Shunyata also expresses a 'letting go'. If you tried to describe that which lay beyond the conventional things we experience as some kind of positive reality (perhaps as God) then it would be possible to crave and try to cling onto that idea of God as a way of escaping from the process of change. Shunyata, by contrast, is simply the recognition that nothing has independent selfhood – nothing can exist on its own, everything is interconnected. In other words – and this is crucial – emptiness is not a 'something' that lies behind phenomena, it is simply a reminder that nothing is independent and self-existing.

see also...

Anatta; Mahayana; Philosophies; Wisdom

Six Realms

Buddhism is concerned with the way the world is experienced, and it often expresses this visually. The third circle on the Wheel of Life shows what are generally referred to as the Six Realms. They appear as separate, isolated worlds, but are generally interpreted as six ways in which the world may be experienced – they are therefore more about psychology than geography. In each of them a Buddha figure appears.

They are:

1 The realm of the gods – depicted as a realm of ease and aesthetic pleasure. To them, the Buddha figure plays the melody of impermanence.

2 The realm of the assuras, or Titans – those who struggle for power. The Buddha has a sword, representing wisdom.

3 The realm of the animals – those who are content with the basic necessities of life and their own creature comforts. The Buddha figure offers a book representing the Dhamma.

4 The hell realms – Buddhism includes the ideas of many different hells, both hot and cold. They do not represent externally imposed states but the internal experience of those dominated by the three poisons of greed, hate and ignorance, leading to despair. The Buddha figure offers ambrosia, giving relief to those who suffer.

5 The realm of the hungry ghosts – traditionally portrayed with knives sticking out of their stomachs, the hungry ghosts are constantly feeding but never satisfied, suffering from the pain inflicted by their own stomachs. The Buddha offers real food and drink.

6 The human realm – often depicted in ways that express creativity. Here, of course, is the realm within which one can follow Buddhist practice.

By showing an image of the Buddha teaching in each realm, it emphasizes that none is a realm from which it is impossible to escape.

see also...

Kamma; Poisons; Re-becoming; Twelve Links

Skandhas

Buddhism teaches that what we conventionally know as the 'self' is constantly changing and comprises of five *skandhas* (heaps or bundles). These are:

1 **Form** (*rupa*) The physical body; constantly changing and dependent for its continued existence on its environment. It includes the sense organs and all that we experience through them. This 'heap' is the whole of physical reality.
2 **Sensations** (*vedana*) Vedana includes the sensations that we receive through the five senses, but also the ideas encountered by the mind. (The mind is regarded as a sixth sense in Buddhist teaching; it encounters a world of ideas and concepts, just as the eye encounters a visible world.)
3 **Perceptions** (*samjna*) As soon as we experience something, we start to conceptualize it, to see it as distinct from other things. We find our way around in the world because of our perceptions. Without them, all we would have is raw feelings or sensations.
4 **Mental formations** (*samskara*) and **impulses** As a result of perceiving things, we relate to them; by finding them either pleasant or unpleasant, we try to experience more or less of them respectively. This skandha includes what we might call our habits – our regular and distinctive pattern of response.
5 **Consciousness** (*vijnana*) This is the skandha that holds the others together. Consciousness allows the arising of sensations, perceptions and mental formations. Each faculty has its own corresponding consciousness (for example, eye consciousness).

In an early scripture, the *Questions of King Milinda*, the self is likened to a chariot made up of various parts, none of which can be identified with the chariot as a whole. In the same way, a Buddhist is invited to analyze himself or herself into the component parts and then recognize that none of them is what might conventionally be called the 'self'.

see also...

Anatta; Samskaras

Skilful Means

Buddhists generally refer to actions as either skilful or unskilful, rather than as good or bad. There are several reasons for this: the first is that actions are related to the person who performs them, and what may be right for one person might be wrong for another; the second that Buddhist morality takes the intention of the person performing the action into account; the third is that actions have consequences (*karma*) and they can therefore be assessed according to whether they produce positive or negative karma for the person who performs them.

Underlying these is the overall sense that Buddhism (unlike religions based on the belief in a God who acts as a law-giver) does not separate the moral significance of actions from the spiritual practice of the person performing them. If a law were given by a god, reward or punishment might be expected to follow depending on whether a person obeyed or disobeyed it. There is no such law-giver in Buddhism. This does not make morality less important within Buddhism, rather it is the refusal to allow absolute and fixed moral laws to lead to either self-satisfaction or despair.

Hence everything is judged in a more flexible way. It is generally termed unskilful if it springs from greed, hatred or ignorance (the three mental poisons), and skilful if from their opposites – love, generosity and wisdom. There is also the sense that there may be occasions when even the precepts may have to be set aside in order to achieve some higher aim. This is the principle of skilful means – knowing what the best thing to do is in any particular situation. In Buddhism, morality, insight and intention are the keywords, rather than obedience.

see also...

Morality; Precepts

Stupas

A stupa is a monument enclosing the ashes or relics of the Buddha or one of his followers. Stupas are called by different names in different areas: Dagobas (Sri Lanka), Pagodas (Burma) and Chortens (Tibet and among Tibetan communities elsewhere). The Buddha's remains, following his own wishes, were divided into eight portions and distributed, and over each of these a stupa was built. Many other stupas were constructed in the following centuries, as a focus for devotion at a time before it became general to produce images of the Buddha.

Stupas believed to contain the relics of Shakyamuni Buddha are located at important Buddhist sites in India and have become places of pilgrimage. There, and elsewhere, it is customary for pilgrims to walk around the stupa in a clockwise direction. Traditionally, each of the four sides of the stupa is taken to represent a moment in the life of Gotama: the east, his birth; the south, his enlightenment; the west, his teaching; and the north, his death. Sometimes these four events are illustrated on the respective sides. In walking around the stupa in a clockwise direction, Buddhist pilgrims follow the life of the Buddha from birth to death.

As well as the major stupas at places of pilgrimage, there are smaller ones built for the remains of other Buddhists, often as a mark of respect by students for their spiritual teacher. The teacher's remains would be distributed to the various monasteries where he taught, and at each place a memorial stupa would be built. At places of pilgrimage, many of these are clustered together around the monastery or shrine.

It is also traditional, following cremation, for the ashes of a Buddhist to be enclosed in a small stupa which is placed on the local shrine, or on a shrine in the family home.

see also...

Chortens; Death

Sutras

A sutra is a text which purports to record the teachings of the Buddha himself. Sutras generally start with the words 'Thus have I heard…' and then give a historical reference to where the Buddha was staying at the time. The Buddha himself left no written material, and these early accounts of his teaching were passed orally for the first 400 years. It is believed that Ananda, who had accompanied the Buddha as his personal assistant for many years, recited all the sutras at the first Council, the gathering of the Buddha's disciples soon after his death.

Other sutras were written long after the death of the Buddha, and there was debate within the Buddhist community about their value. Some of them form the scriptures of Mahayana Buddhism. Their style and ideas are, in places, quite different from the early sutras, but Mahayana Buddhists argue that they reflect teachings of the Buddha, and that those teachings were too difficult for his immediate followers to understand, but were preserved in oral tradition until an appropriate time for them to be revealed. This fits in with the general Buddhist idea that everything should be appropriate for particular people and circumstances – so a teaching is revealed when people are ready for it.

As well as the sutras, there are Shastras, which are expositions of the Buddha's teaching by his disciples. These tend to be a more systematic presentation of ideas, unlike the early sutras, which generally record dialogues between the Buddha and various people who come to ask his advice.

Some sutras – particularly the great Mahayana ones, such as *The Lotus Sutra* – are essentially compilations of teaching, and some parts may have been written centuries after others. Those concerned about historical detail and authorship might be tempted to discard later material in favour of early texts. For early Buddhists, however, the Dhamma was timeless, so it really did not matter when a particular teaching was written down.

see also...

Pali; Scriptures

Tantra

Tantra is the term used for a movement within both Buddhism and Hinduism that flourished from about 500 CE and which brought into the practice of those religions ritual and magical elements that were probably of ancient origin.

Tantric practice involved three things:

1 Reciting particular phrases and formulae which, rather like magic spells, were believed to be powerful.

2 Acting out ritual dances and gestures, which have the effect of involving body and emotions in religion.

3 In conjunction with the first two things, the visualization of oneself as one of the Bodhisattvas or other deities.

One might say that, for Tantra, a person becomes involved with ritual and with visualization, in order to experience what it is like to be enlightened. In other words, it is an imaginative entering into the very thing that one wants to become. An important aspect of tantra is connected with sexuality. In Hindu thought, the female power shown in the person of the goddesses, or consorts of the gods, is termed *shakti*. There is a balance between male and female. In Buddhist tantra there is a similar balance, shown in the tantric Yab-yum images. The most basic of these shows the sexual embrace of Vajradhara (the vajra holder) and Prajnaparamitar (the perfection of wisdom). In all these sexual images, the male represents skilful action or morality and the female, wisdom. Some tantric practitioners probably used their wives, or sometimes prostitutes, in order to act out rituals involving intercourse, but within Buddhism, the physical gave way to the symbolic, or was confined to the realm of visualization.

Two key features of Tantra are that it seeks a quick way to get insight, compared with years of patient meditation, and that it is generally performed only under the instructions of a guru. Elements of Tantra found their way into the Mahayana Buddhism of the Far East, but it is mainly found in Tibetan Buddhism.

see also...

Tibetan Buddhism; Visualization

Tara

The historical Buddha accepted that men and women were equally capable of following his teaching. When Buddhism became influenced by devotional traditions and started to use a multiplicity of Buddha and Bodhisattva images representing aspects of the enlightened mind, it was natural that there should be females as well as males. Indeed, within Tibetan Buddhism, each of the Buddhas in the mandala has a consort, and the female figures are particularly associated with wisdom, notably Prajnaparamita. Tara is a female Bodhisattva, prominent particularly in Tibetan Buddhism. Her name means 'one who carries over', and she is therefore seen as one who will help one cross the waters of samsara (this world of change and suffering). She embodies compassion. One of the stories about her origin is that she was born from a tear that was shed by the Bodhisattva Avalokiteshvara as he contemplated the impossible task of saving all creatures from suffering. The tear fell to earth and formed a lake out of which there grew a lotus, which opened to reveal the goddess Tara.

There are different images of Tara, the most popular ones being either green or white. Since she is seen as seeking to save all beings from suffering, she is sometimes referred to as the 'mother of all Buddhas and Bodhisattvas'.

It is customary to see all the Buddha figures as having passed through a succession of lifetimes through which they have prepared themselves for their present task. And this applies to the more imaginative, archetypal images as well as to the historical Buddha. The former lives are seen as a way of describing character. In the case of Tara, the tradition is that she chose to be born in a female form for each of her lives, in order to be of special help to those who find they can identify better with a female.

see also...

Avalokiteshvara; Bodhisattva; Thankas

Teachers

For Buddhist practice to be effective, it is generally argued that you should be guided by a teacher, rather than practice on your own. There are two reasons for this. The first is to ensure that you have understood the teachings in a way that is appropriate to your own situation, since teachings are not fixed or universally applicable, but are aimed to be understood and applied individually. Secondly, some of the spiritual techniques – especially in vipassana (insight) meditation – are suited to particular psychological types, and it is part of the tradition of Buddhist spiritual guidance that a teacher assesses which practices are likely to be of benefit to each individual.

In Tibetan Buddhism, senior teachers are called *lamas*, and each stands within a particular tradition, in what is termed a lineage. The lineage is the succession of spiritual teachers who have handed down their tradition from one to another. Tibetan Buddhists will sometimes visualize senior teachers of their lineage arranged on a family tree, along with their own personal teacher.

The lineage is seen as important, as guaranteeing the authenticity of one's teacher. Throughout Tibetan Buddhism there is a certain amount of competition within and between traditions. Lamas need not be monks; qualified lay teachers are also termed lamas. *Guru* is the general term for a spiritual teacher and it is used particularly within the Tibetan tradition. There is also the term *geshe*, which refers to someone who has been through a long period of monastic training (traditionally 25 years, but sometimes less these days). A geshe may or may not be a lama.

The actual content of what is taught varies considerably. Although Buddhism does not depend on creeds or require practitioners to subscribe to set beliefs, there are many lists and set ways of presenting Buddhist Dhamma, and these may be learnt by heart. In some traditions whole portions of scriptures are memorized and recited, in others (for example, Zen) the tradition is passed on between teacher and student without being linked to any particular scripture.

see also...

Dhamma; Tibetan Buddhism

Thankas

One of the most remarkable features of Buddhism is the stark visual contrast between the places of worship of its different branches. Enter the meditation hall of a Zen monastery, and all is absolutely plain. Enter a Tibetan shrine, and you are surrounded by a wealth of colour and imagery, as well as sound and action.

A prominent feature of the devotional side of Buddhism, contributing to the richness of its shrines, are *thankas.* These are wall hangings, depicting Buddhas and Bodhisattvas. Unlike mandalas, which are often produced for a particular festival and may then be destroyed, thankas generally remain in the shrineroom as aids to devotion. They also serve as a teaching aid, by displaying a range of symbols which together express the qualities of the particular Buddha or Bodhisattva figure portrayed.

Some thankas are huge, and are displayed out of doors at major festivals. They form a particularly appropriate backdrop for processions and the acting out of dance dramas.

A thanka displayed above a small shrine

see also...

Tara; Tibetan Buddhism; Worship

Theravada

Of the early branches of the Buddhist Sangha, the Theravada is the only one to have survived to the present day. The name means 'Tradition of the Elders' and represents one of the most conservative forms of Buddhism. The earliest Buddhist scriptures – the Pali Canon – were preserved and handed down within the Theravada tradition. Theravada is sometimes referred to as South East Asian Buddhism because it spread from India to Sri Lanka and other south east Asian countries, and there became the dominant tradition. It is now found worldwide and claims to be the form of Buddhism that keeps most closely to the earliest traditions of the Buddha.

In Theravada, there is a pronounced emphasis on the monastic Sangha, and the way of life of a monk or nun is regarded as the Buddhist ideal. There is a good balance in traditional Theravada countries between monks and lay people, the latter providing the former with foods and other requirements, and in turn receiving teaching and spiritual guidance. Theravada Buddhism seems, superficially, to place its emphasis on individual striving towards enlightenment (in order to become an *arhat*), and as such is sometimes contrasted with the Mahayana vision of the Bodhisattva, who seeks the happiness and enlightenment of all. This traditionally led the Theravada to be referred to as Hinayana or 'small vehicle'. However, it is clear that the whole of the Buddhist path – Theravada as much as Mahayana – aims at the welfare and happiness of the many. To seek enlightenment for selfish reasons is a contradiction in terms and a spiritual impossibility. However, it remains true that the Theravada retains a formal structure and hierarchy which (to some outside that tradition) may appear restricting.

see also...

Diversity; Hinayana; Pali

Tibetan Buddhism

Buddhism reached Tibet in about 700 CE, long after it had spread further north through China and the Far East. As a result, the form of Buddhism that took root there included the more recent developments of Buddhism within India. By about the fourth century, mantras, mudras, mandalas and the depicting of deities were all found within some Mahayana circles. These gradually became systematized into what was to become Vajrayana, the third of the Buddist 'vehicles'. It was this rich blend of Buddhist traditions that found its way into Tibet.

By the eleventh century, Buddhism was effectively destroyed in its native India (in part as a result of Muslim invasions and the destruction of its great monastic and educational centres), and it was therefore primarily in Tibet that the Vajrayana was preserved.

There are four schools of Tibetan Buddhism, each with a particular lineage and tradition. The Kagyu, headed by the Karmapa, has spread to Europe, the United States and the Far East. The present Karmapa (the seventeenth), a boy aged 14, escaped from Tibet – where he was effectively imprisoned by the Chinese – at the end of 1999, and made his way overland to Nepal and thence into India. Another school, the Gelugpa, is particularly well known because it is headed by the Dalai Lama, who was the effective ruler of Tibet until the Chinese invasion.

During the last 50 years, Tibetan Buddhism has been transformed largely because of the Chinese invasion of Tibet and its attempts to stamp out Buddhism there. With the escape from Tibet of the Dalai Lama in 1959, and the Karmapa in 1999, the focus of Tibetan Buddhism has shifted outside Tibet itself. Previously locked within a very remote and traditional cultural setting, it is now one of the most widely known forms of Buddhism in the West as well as the East.

see also...

Diversity; Tantra; Tulkus

Trikaya Doctrine

How can one relate the historical Buddha to all the Buddha images used in worship and to the idea of a universal Buddha nature? One attempt to do this is the Mahayana teaching about the 'three bodies' of the Buddha – the *trikaya*:

1 **The Nirmanakaya** This stands for the physical form of the Buddha, seen in the most straightforward way as the one who teaches.
2 **The Dharmakaya** This is the 'body' of truth as taught by the Buddha. In other words, if a person becomes enlightened, he or she is aware of their own 'Buddha nature' and in a sense becomes Buddha. The Dharmakaya represents the absoulte reality, or Buddhahood, to which the physical and historical Buddha pointed.
3 **The Sambhogakaya** Between the two extremes of the meaning of 'Buddha' given above – one concrete and the other abstract – the Mahayana developed a third 'body' for the Buddha, termed the Sambhogakaya. This is the level of images, represented, for example, by the many Buddha and Bodhisattva figures in shrines. These are clearly not the same as the historical Buddha and nobody expects them to appear in some physical form. Yet they attempt to make the abstract truth of Buddhahood more immediate and understandable. They also enable emotional engagement in the process of worship and understanding.

There is no sense that the Buddha is divided. It is simply that the Mahayana see him as being experienced in all three different ways. In a sense, for the Mahayana, everything is Buddha, everything has a Buddha nature. But it's not easy to see, and therefore the abstract reality needs to be communicated in more accessible ways. The various images of the Sambhogakaya, each with its own particular qualities, seek to do this.

see also...

Buddha Nature; Mahayana

Tulkus

Generally speaking, Buddhist teaching does not encourage speculation about the prospect of future births, and in any case it is argued that there is no permanent self that could move from one life to the next. However, within Tibetan Buddhism, it is believed that the most spiritually advanced lamas can choose to return again as a human being in order to continue their work of compassion, with the aim of leading all beings to escape the sufferings of samsara.

Thus, shortly after a senior lama dies, an enquiry is made to find a child, born at the appropriate time, who might be the new incarnation of the life that was the former lama. Such a new incarnation of a lama is termed a 'Tulku'. In this way, it is believed that there is a continuity between one lama's teaching and the next.

The Dalai Lama is an example of just such a Tulku. As a child he was put through various tests in order to ascertain whether he had any knowledge of, for example, particular possessions belonging to the previous Dalai Lama that would suggest that he was his next incarnation. A child, once declared a Tulku, is trained for his future office and is treated with the respect due to an adult lama.

Much has been made of this feature of Tibetan Buddhism, for example in the film *The Little Buddha*. The importance of the idea of the Tulku is related to the central place given to the lama, and the need for a spiritual guide with Tibetan Buddhism.

see also...

Bardo States; Death; Tibetan Buddhism

Twelve Links (Nidanas)

The process of conditioned co-production (interconnectedness) is central to Buddhism, and one expression of it, termed the *nidanas*, is set out in the form of 12 traditional images, set as the outermost ring of the Wheel of Life. Starting with a blind man, representing ignorance, and a potter expressing the actions that are created while in that state of ignorance, the nidanas trace the arising of sense experience, its encounter with the world around it, and its consequent contact with and clinging to experience, leading to further birth and death.

The intention is to show that, within the world of samsara, each of these arises only with the previous one as its condition – in other words, it is only on the basis of ignorance that the whole process is carried forward. The nidanas form a basic way of looking at experience and response, a cyclic pattern that can only be broken by a refusal to grasp at that which is experienced.

The psychological implication of the cyclic nature of the process is that one cannot annihilate the past (like it or not, it has been the cause of the present), nor can one create an eternal or perfect future (the attempt to do so always leading to frustration and further suffering – *dukkha*). Awareness of the nidanas is an awareness of a flow of life within which one is a creative participant, shaped by the past and shaping the future, and interconnected in the present with everything else that exists.

There is another set of 12 positive nidana links, expressing progress in the spiritual life away from suffering and towards enlightenment. They are: suffering, faith, delight, rapture, tranquility, bliss, concentration, knowledge and vision of things as they really are, withdrawal, dispassion, freedom and knowledge of the destruction of the taints.

see also...

Interconectedness; Kamma; Wheel of Life

Vajra

Vajra can have two meanings – 'diamond' and 'thunderbolt'. It gives its name to the Vajrayana branch of Buddhism, found particularly in the Tibetan tradition, a tradition which emphasizes the transformation and direction of human energies in the pursuit of enlightenment. The vajra is also a physical object used in Buddhist ritual. It comprises a central sphere, out of which there emerge two stylized lotus flowers from opposite poles, and from each of these there come five spokes branching out and then meeting at a point.

Vajra

The central sphere represents the whole of reality. The lotus flowers represent two opposite ways of interpreting reality – one positive and one negative. From the negative lotus the five spokes represent the five *skandhas* (elements within the self) but also the five poisons (infatuation, hatred, conceit, passion and envy). Those from the positive lotus represent the five Buddhas of the mandala, each of which offers a particular form of wisdom to counter one of the poisons. Thus, the energy that can produce the poisons can also be transformed to produce the wisdoms.

A key feature of this interpretation of the vajra is that there are not separate worlds or realities – one good and the other bad. Rather, there is a single reality which gives rise to both good and bad, and that the energy that produces the one may be transformed into that which produces the other. As the symbol of transforming power, the vajra may be held in the hand during rituals, or it may appear as a motif in shrines, representing the determination of the follower and transforming power of the Buddhist path.

see also...

Lotus; Skandhas; Tantra; Tibetan Buddhism

Vajrayana

Within Buddhism, there are three broad 'vehicles', or ways of following the Buddhist path: the early form, sometimes referred to as the Hinayama (small vehicle) and represented now by the Theravada; the Mahayana (great vehicle) which includes the Far Eastern forms of Buddhism; and the Vajrayana (diamond vehicle), represented now mainly by Tibetan Buddhism.

Vajrayana Buddhism uses Tantric and other practices in order to strike through to one's fundamental nature, often using ritual, and, what in the West would generally be termed supernatural powers, or magic. A key feature of vajrayana is the transformation of energy. Thus, for example, the Tantra (both Buddhist and non-Buddhist) makes much of utilizing female power (*Shakti*) and of seeing sexuality as a union of male and female principles, as an expression of and vehicle for spiritual transformation, by the union of wisdom and skilful action.

The visible side of Vajrayana Buddhism is quite different from the other yanas. It uses ritual actions and symbols, and its worship (*puja*) can be bold and colourful. It engages the emotions and seeks to harness their power for spiritual purposes. With a great range of rituals and meditations on Buddhas and Bodhisattvas, some expressing anger and energy, the Vajrayana tradition has emphasized the need for guidance in one's practice from an experienced teacher – recognizing that some vajrayana practices can be destructive if used wrongly.

At one time the Tantric elements of the Vajrayana were kept secret. That is less true today, and the Vajrayana as a whole is far better known worldwide, particularly because of the exile of Tibetan lamas from their homeland.

see also...

Diversity; Tantra; Tibetan Buddhism; Vajra

Viharas

In the days of the Buddha, it was customary for ascetics and spiritual teachers (generally known as *shramaneras*) to travel around with bands of followers, staying for periods of time in parks and other open areas near centres of population. Lay followers would come out to hear them teach and also to provide them with food and other necessities. The Buddha followed this same pattern. For much of the year, his followers were sent out to preach the Dhamma, but they gathered together for three months each year for the 'rains retreat', during the rainy season, when travel was difficult. The places used for the annual retreat, and also those where they stayed while on their travels, were known as *viharas* (literally 'resting places').

Since the Buddha and his followers had no material resources of their own, the viharas were given and established for them by wealthy lay followers. As time went on, these viharas became the basis for more settled monastic communities, conveniently located just outside towns and villages. Monks from the vihara would receive support from lay followers mainly in the form of food, offered during the daily alms round, but more generally in terms of establishing and equipping the vihara. In return, the monks would teach and act as an example for the lay Buddhists to follow.

Today, viharas provide a range of facilities for lay people. It is to the vihara that people go for ceremonies, major festivals, to make retreats and to receive teaching. One tradition, particularly within the Theravada, is for a young person to spend some time in a vihara, getting a taste for the monastic life. For most, of course, this will be for only a matter of days or weeks, but it is regarded as a coming-of-age opportunity within the Buddhist community, and a means of strengthening the bond between the monastic and lay communities.

see also...

Monasticism; Sangha

Vinaya

This, the second of the 'three baskets' of the Pali canon, is the term used for the rules of the monastic Sangha. The core element in this is the *Pratimoksha* (*Pattimokka* in Pali), the set of between 227 and 253 rules that are read out every two weeks when the monastic community meets together. These vinaya rules are very similar in all versions, and are therefore probably very old, originating at a time before the different groups separated off from one another.

The vinaya sets down the day-to-day rules for the running of the monastic community. Because the monastic Sangha is so important within Buddhism, both in terms of its organization, its leading of public worship (*puja*) and meditation, and also its preservation and recitation of the scriptures, the rules of the vinaya have assumed a greater importance within Buddhism than the equivalent rules in other religions.

Some divisions within the Sangha come as a result of different interpretation of rules, rather than differences of belief. For example, one of the key issues discussed at the Second Council was whether or not monks should be allowed to handle money. The vinaya also sets out what should happen in the case of serious breaches of the monastic rules. In four cases (having sex, theft, murder, and making false claims to have supernatural powers) the person concerned is expelled from the monastic Sangha, since these things are considered incompatible with their monastic life. Lesser offences may require a monk or nun to be excluded from the Sangha for a period of time, or to make a confession of their faults.

The vinaya rules do not negate the general Buddhist principle of adopting precepts rather than obeying rules, and of emphasizing intention when considering morality. They are simply provided to enable the monastic community to live and work together, to ensure that no scandal brings the community into disrepute, and to maintain an environment which is conducive to spiritual practice.

see also...

Monasticism; Pali

Vipassana meditation

It is one thing to have a mind that is calm and controlled and able to focus without being distracted. In itself, that is of great benefit, and is the aim of Samatha meditation. It can lead a person out of the illusion of ordinary experience. However, Buddhism seeks to achieve more than that, and to gain deep insight into the nature of reality. The techniques used for seeking this are termed *vipassana* or 'insight' meditation.

For example, Buddhism teaches that everything is interconnected and that the idea of a separate, independent self is an illusion. It is relatively easy to get an intellectual grasp of that, but how might one come to experience and 'feel' it as a constant reality? One technique is to imagine the different elements (*skandhas*) that make up the self, and to see each of them being shared with the rest of the world, so that one does not seek to hold on to or become identified with them. Thus, for example, our physical bodies are made up of material that is not particularly 'ours', but has been gathered together, through food and drink, from the external world. How can I identify as 'mine' a physical body that is, in a sense, only borrowed?

In general, vipassana meditation should only be practised under the guidance of a personal teacher, as the meditation used needs to be carefully selected to match the needs of the practitioner. Thus, for example, one of the more extreme forms of meditation is on the stages of decomposition of a corpse, a rather gruesome practice (not prescribed for everyone) which aims at detachment from concern with the physical body. Whilst this might be valuable for making a skilled practitioner even more aware of the transient nature of life, is likely to produce in a beginner a sense of morbid curiosity and depression that would not be at all helpful.

see also...

Meditation; Visualizations; Wisdom

Visualizations

Try shutting your eyes and thinking of nothing: it's very difficult, the mind keeps filling up with images. One of the problems with simple activities like focusing on the breathing is that the mind is constantly being distracted by thoughts and fantasies. There is one aspect of Buddhist practice that makes use of his however: visualization.

Many forms of meditation involve looking at an object (either literally, or in imagination) until the image can be formed clearly in the mind's eye, then set aside, then formed again at will. Visualization goes one step beyond this. Here, a person forms an image and then gives careful attention to it. The many images of Buddhas and Bodhisattvas are elaborate and full of symbolism – both in terms of colour, appearance, posture, clothing and items being held. A great deal of Buddhist teaching may be conveyed symbolically in this way. In visualization practice, a person sees such a Buddha figure in the mind's eye, and then gives careful attention to its details. In a sense, the figure 'comes alive' for the practitioner, who may actually enter into a kind of mental dialogue with him or her.

An aspect of visualization, particular in Tantric Buddhism, is to visualize oneself as a Buddha or Bodhisattva. To the outsider, this may seem rather egocentric. To the person practising in this way, it is an imaginative attempt to understand what it would be like to be enlightened. In other words, rather like some Western techniques for self-development, you imagine that you have already achieved the desired quality. Now, how does that feel? What is it like to look at the world as a being filled with compassion or wisdom? The effect of this is to help a person cultivate in reality the quality experienced during the visualization.

see also...

Images; Meditation; Tantra

Wesak

In Theravada Buddhism, the birth, enlightenment and death of the Buddha are celebrated on the same day – the full moon day of the second month of the Indian year, *Vaishakha*, which is *Wesak* in Sinhalese. The festival is therefore named after the month in which it falls.

Temples are decorated for the festival, and both temples and homes may have lanterns burning after dark – using light as a symbol of the Buddha's enlightenment. This is particularly the case in Sri Lanka, where Wesak is characterized almost as a festival of light, and there may be processions through the streets with lanterns. As at other festivals, people come to spend time at a temple, listening to talks on the Dhamma or sitting in meditation. Many will bring elaborate food offerings for the monks – as an expression of gratitude for the Dhamma and as a way of displaying the quality of generosity (*dana*).

Wesak can be celebrated at many different levels. Some will send Wesak cards to one another or have it as a day of family celebration. Others will treat it in a more religious and serious way, taking on extra precepts for the day, and spending the time in meditation. Still others regard the festival as relatively unimportant. In general, there is an ambivalent attitude to festivals in Buddhism. On the one hand they serve a useful purpose, on the other, the real business of striving towards enlightenment is a personal quest which takes place every day and to which festivals and other external observances are largely irrelevant.

As always, Buddhism is flexible about if and how festivals should be celebrated. Most Buddhists are happy to regard all externals of the festival as a useful reminder of the key event in the life of the Buddha, and as an opportunity to reaffirm their own commitment to following his path.

see also...

Festivals

Western Buddhism

From its origins in Northern India, Buddhism spread through South East Asia, the Far East and the Himalayan region during the first 1500 years of its existence. By then, Hinayana, Mahayana and Vajrayana traditions had taken root in the different geographical areas. As Buddhism spread, so it changed, taking into account the needs of the cultures it encountered.

Today, Buddhism is practised throughout the world. It spread to Western Europe and North America mainly during the twentieth century, although individuals were aware of Buddhism long before that. By the nineteenth century, many academics and historians, exploring oriental culture, started to study Buddhist teachings, and scriptures started to become available in translation. This, of course, was aided by the British political involvement in India and the Far East. Contact between the USA and the Far East led to increasing numbers of Mahayana Buddhists, particularly Chinese, living and practising their religion in the USA.

Then, following the Chinese Invasion of Tibet in 1950, many Tibetan lamas moved to the West and continued to teach and establish themselves both among exiled Tibetan communities, but also making Tibetan Buddhism available for Westerners.

Today, all three branches of Buddhism are practised in the West, both among expatriate communities from traditionally Buddhist countries, and by Westerners. Some groups have consciously adapted their practice and language to meet the needs of Westerners. There are also new Buddhist groups that have developed in the West, based on the earlier traditions. These include The Samatha Trust, which specializes in teaching meditation and has its roots in the Thai Theravadin tradition, and the Friends of the Western Buddhist Order, which takes from all the earlier traditions, but is criticized by some mainstream Buddhists for its unconventional approach to moral, social and organisational issues.

see also...

Diversity

Wheel of Life

The Wheel of Life is a spiritual map, expressing the various conditions within which people may find themselves in this world (the world of Samsara, or change), and the process by which change is brought about.

At the hub of the wheel are three animals: a cock (representing greed), a snake (representing hatred) and a pig (representing ignorance). They are seen linked, as though feeding on one another. They represent the three poisons that keep the wheel of Samsara turning. Around this is a circle within which, on one side, people are falling downward, and on the other they are ascending. This represents the progress or otherwise of people, depending upon their *kamma* (*karma*), or actions.

The next major circle is divided into six parts, each representing a 'realm' within which a person may find him or herself. They represent: the heavenly realm, the world of the angry gods, the animal realm, the hell realm, the realm of the hungry ghosts, and finally the human realm. In each of these there is depicted a Buddha teaching.

The outermost ring of the wheel shows the 12 nidanas, or steps illustrating the process by which ignorance leads to continued birth and death. Behind the wheel, Yama, the monstrous god of impermanence and death is seen with the wheel in his jaws.

see also...

Kamma; Poisons; Six Realms; Twelve Links

Wisdom

A key feature of Buddhist wisdom is to find the middle way between the perceived errors of eternalism and nihilism. In other words, to hold that some things in this life are unchangeable and of permanent value, or to hold that nothing is of any significance or value. Each of these are seen as a *micchaditthi* (wrong view). Wisdom comes with seeing all things as interconnected and having a reality and value that arises in spite of their temporary nature.

At his enlightenment, the Buddha was described as gaining an awareness of the way in which all things came into and passed out of existence – the great interconnected stream of reality. That vision, and all that springs from it – notably an awareness of oneself as also changing, shaped by causes and conditions, and therefore capable of taking responsibility for and directing that change – is at the heart of Buddhist wisdom.

Buddhists sometimes make the distinction between conventional truth (*samvrti satya*) and absolute truth (*paramarthika satya*). This is illustrated by the view of the self. In ordinary speech, we refer to ourselves, and we know what we mean by that. I can also speak about 'my book' or 'my car', and know to what that refers. At a deeper level, however, I know that there is nothing about that book that makes it 'mine', and that I am just a temporary collection of ever-changing atoms, thoughts and emotions and habits. On the other hand, one cannot, for practical purposes, deal with absolute truth all the time.

see also...

Anatta; Middle Way; Philosophies

Worship (Puja)

It is important to remember that Buddhism does not have the concept of a creator God. Although there are many references to gods in the scriptures, these refer to the conventional belief that there are many realms inhabited to beings generally called 'devas'. Although these are said to live in a state of pleasure and refinement, they are still subject to the laws of kamma (*karma*), and do not have the same status as God in Western religion. Therefore, when Buddhists perform *puja*, or worship, they are not praying to a god in the Western sense.

Essentially, Buddhist worship comprises making offerings and paying respect to the Buddha and his many representations in the form of Buddha and Bodhisattva images that are found on shrines. Worship is an attempt to enter imaginatively into the qualities expressed by the Buddha image, and to engage the emotions in the expression of gratitude for the Buddhist path.

The Buddha insisted that one of the fetters that prevented spiritual development was the reliance of rites and ceremonies. It is therefore important that Buddhists should not think that some benefit will automatically be gained by performing a ceremony. Whatever power there is in a puja comes from the effect it has upon the mind of the person who takes part. A puja is a form of spiritual activity, parallel to meditation and is judged – as is meditation – on the gradual transformation of a person from unskilful to skilful mental states and habitual dispositions.

Worship is particularly prominent in Tibetan Buddhism, where there is great emphasis on ritual, with colourful robes, thankas and music and movement. Zen Buddhism, by contrast, has little of this.

see also...

Pure Land Buddhism; Shrines; Tantra

Za-zen

Za-zen is the basic meditation practice of Zen Buddhists and is particularly important within the Soto Zen tradition. The practitioner sits facing the wall of the Zendo (meditation room), so as to minimize distractions. Hands are placed on the lap, resting one on top of the other, palms turned upwards (the 'meditation', or *dhyana* mudra), and it is usual to meditate with the eyes remaining open, or partly open, which helps the meditator to keep alert and focused in the present moment. (It is easier to daydream when your eyes are closed.)

As with other forms of Samatha meditation, the mind is progressively cleared of distracting thoughts. Traditionally, when monks meditate together in their Zendo, one of their number walks up and down carrying a long flat piece of wood, like a paddle. If any of the meditating monks appears to be sleepy, he is given a sharp tap across the shoulders.

There is no set period for meditation. Monks are generally able to meditate for longer than is possible for lay people with other commitments. The essential thing is the effectiveness in preparing the mind for an immediate awareness of the present, a state in which all discursive thought ceases, and one becomes simply aware.

During long sessions of sitting meditation, monks may stay alert by having periods of walking meditation between their za-zen periods of sitting. They move slowly and in full awareness of body, mind and surroundings, trying not to become distracted from the progress made in the meditation.

Za-zen is not fundamentally different as a practice from Samatha meditation in older forms of Buddhism. Both aim to still the jumble of conventional thoughts, allowing the mind to become single-pointed. Zen has developed this particular approach making it clear that it does not aim at gaining anything, but simply being aware of what is already fundamentally true about oneself and everything else – a pure seeing.

see also...

Meditation; Zen

Zen

Zen is the Japanese for 'meditation'. Zen Buddhists see all people as potentially enlightened, but as blind to the fact. It therefore uses meditation and other practices to awaken a person to his or her own enlightenment and thus achieve a pure seeing into the true nature of everything.

Enlightenment is not seen as something to be gained in the distant future, but to be experienced now through meditation in moments of insight, termed *satori*.

There are two basic forms of Zen: Rinzai and Soto. Rinzai Zen emphasizes the immediate possibility of enlightenment, and tries to break down conventional thinking by using koans, questions that make no sense in terms of conventional logic, and mondos, stories designed to produce insight. The aim is to achieve sudden, pure awareness (satori). Soto Zen places greater emphasis on the slow and systematic approach offered by sitting meditation (*Za-zen*), although it also uses koans.

Zen has had a profound impact on the arts. Activities such as archery and flower arranging can, for Zen practitioners, become vehicles for spiritual development. The essential thing is to stay absolutely in the present moment, letting go of aspirations that may limit a person's present view by concentrating on the future. Zen has contributed a great deal to Japanese culture. Gardens of raked sand reflect the calm of meditation. The tea ceremony, where great attention is given to each action, is an example of Zen attentiveness. The short poem, or Haiku, illustrates the simplicity and restraint of Zen. In a strictly limited number of syllables, the Haiku seeks to give an insight or evoke a sense of deeper awareness. Zen claims to be a tradition passed down orally by the Buddha to his chosen followers. It is therefore based on the relationship with a qualified teacher who stands within that ongoing tradition, rather than on the study of scriptures. With its rejection of scriptures and logical patterns of thinking, Zen may seem somewhat anarchic and unconventional.

see also...

Satori; Za-zen

Further Reading

E Conze Cassirer, (1951), *Buddhism*. OUP.
Denise Cush, (1994), *Buddhism*. Hodder and Stoughton.
Clive Erricker, (1995), *Teach Yourself Buddhism*. Hodder and Stoughton.
S.K. Hookham, (1991), *The Buddha Within*. State University New York Press.
D.J. Kalupahana, (1992), *History of Buddhist Philosophy*. University of Hawaii Press.
Phra Prayudh Payutto, (1995), *Buddhadhamma*. State University New York Press.
Andrew Skilton, (1994), *Concise History of Buddhism, A*. Windhorse.
Walpola Rahula, (1959), *What The Buddha Taught*. Oneworld Publication.

The extracts from the *Dhammapada* are taken from the translation by J. Mascaro, Penguin Classics, 1973.

Also available in the series

TY 101 Key Ideas: Astronomy	Jim Breithaupt	0 340 78214 5
TY 101 Key Ideas: Ecology	Paul Mitchell	0 340 78209 9
TY 101 Key Ideas: Evolution	Morton Jenkins	0 340 78210 2
TY 101 Key Ideas: Existentialism	George Myerson	0 340 78152 1
TY 101 Key Ideas: Genetics	Morton Jenkins	0 340 78211 0
TY 101 Key Ideas: Philosophy	Paul Oliver	0 340 78029 0
TY 101 Key Ideas: Psychology	Dave Robinson	0 340 78155 6